ISO 9001:2008
for Small and
Medium-Sized
Businesses

Denise E. Robitaille's other books include:

The Corrective Action Handbook

Corrective Action for the Software Industry

Managing Supplier-Related Processes

The Management Review Handbook

The Preventive Action Handbook

Root Cause Analysis: Basic Tools and Techniques

Document Control: A Simple Guide to Managing Documentation

Also available from ASQ Quality Press:

A Practical Field Guide for ISO 9001:2008
Erik Valdemar Myhrberg

ISO 9001:2008 Explained, Third Edition
Charles A. Cianfrani, John E. "Jack" West, and Joseph J. Tsiakals

ISO Lesson Guide 2008: Pocket Guide to ISO 9001-2008, Third Edition
J. P. Russell and Dennis R. Arter

ISO 9001:2008 Internal Audits Made Easy: Tools, Techniques and Step-By-Step Guidelines for Successful Internal Audits, Second Edition
Ann W. Phillips

Process Driven Comprehensive Auditing: A New Way to Conduct ISO 9001:2008 Internal Audits, Second Edition
Paul C. Palmes

ISO 9001:2008 Interpretive Guide for the Design and Construction Project Team (e-Book)
Prepared by members of the ASQ Design and Construction Division and edited by John R. Broomfield

How to Audit the Process-Based QMS
Dennis R. Arter, John E. (Jack) West, and Charles A. Cianfrani

Quality Audits for Improved Performance, Third Edition
Dennis R. Arter

To request a complimentary catalog of ASQ Quality Press publications, call 800-248-1946, or visit our Web site at http://www.asq.org/quality-press.

ISO 9001:2008 for Small and Medium-Sized Businesses

Second Edition

Denise E. Robitaille

ASQ Quality Press
Milwaukee, Wisconsin

American Society for Quality, Quality Press, Milwaukee 53203
© 2011 by ASQ
All rights reserved. Published 2010
Printed in the United States of America
16 15 14 13 12 11 10   5 4 3 2 1

Library of Congress Cataloging-in-Publication Data

Robitaille, Denise E., 1952–.
  ISO 9001:2008 for small and medium-sized businesses / Denise E.
Robitaille. — 2nd ed.
      p. cm.
    Prev. ed. had title: ISO 9001:2000 for small and medium-sized businesses.
    Includes index.
    ISBN 978-0-87389-792-1 (alk. paper)
  1. ISO 9001 Standard.   2. Quality assurance.   3. Quality control.
I. Robitaille, Denise E. ISO 9001:2000 for small and medium-sized
businesses.   II. Title.

    TS156.6.R64 2010
    658.4'013—dc22   2010028236

Publisher: William A. Tony
Acquisitions Editor: Matt Meinholz
Project Editor: Paul O'Mara
Production Administrator: Randall Benson

ASQ Mission: The American Society for Quality advances individual, organizational, and community excellence worldwide through learning, quality improvement, and knowledge exchange.

Attention Bookstores, Wholesalers, Schools, and Corporations: ASQ Quality Press books, video, audio, and software are available at quantity discounts with bulk purchases for business, educational, or instructional use. For information, please contact ASQ Quality Press at 800-248-1946, or write to ASQ Quality Press, P.O. Box 3005, Milwaukee, WI 53201-3005.

To place orders or to request a free copy of the ASQ Quality Press Publications Catalog, including ASQ membership information, call 800-248-1946. Visit our Web site at http://www.asq.org/quality-press.

 Printed on acid-free paper

Quality Press
600 N. Plankinton Avenue
Milwaukee, Wisconsin 53203
Call toll free 800-248-1946
Fax 414-272-1734
www.asq.org
http://www.asq.org/quality-press
http://standardsgroup.asq.org
E-mail: authors@asq.org

Contents

List of Figures and Tables

Preface

This handbook was developed to help small and medium-sized organizations better understand ISO 9001:2008. It is intended to facilitate implementation and improvement. The establishment, implementation, and maintenance of an ISO 9001–compliant quality management system (QMS) should allow the organization to experience multiple benefits beyond the achievement of certification. Organizations should also see improvements in the quality of products, customer satisfaction, and process effectiveness—all of which ultimately have a positive impact on the bottom line.

For those readers whose organizations have already established a QMS, this handbook will serve to reinforce good practices and lead to a better understanding of the intent and value of some of the requirements of ISO 9001. Since this handbook is especially focused on small and medium-sized organizations, the examples provided will have greater applicability and will enhance comprehension, again resulting in increased value.

Many organizations have also implemented sector-specific standards based on ISO 9001. Examples of QMS standards based on ISO 9001 include AS9100 (for aviation, space, and defense), ISO/TS 16949 (for automotive), ISO 13485 (for medical devices), and ISO 17025 (for laboratory accreditation). This handbook should be equally useful to these organizations in understanding the requirements that are common to all of these standards.

In 2008, a minor revision was issued to ISO 9001. It is not necessary to have an understanding of the distinctions between ISO 9001:2008 and any previous version in order to use this handbook.

Terminology will be discussed in Chapter 4; however, there are two terms that bear particular note, and their use should be clarified from the onset.

The word *product* is intended to mean the output of a series of processes that is delivered to a customer. This may include service in those cases where an organization's "product" is a service. Some examples might include transportation, training, after-market servicing of a sold product, financial portfolio management, and healthcare. Note that in each case, the products sound more like activities than what we traditionally think of as products—that is, tangible goods. ISO 9001 has grown and diversified. There has been an explosion in the number of organizations providing service-type products that are required to conform to international QMS standards. In this handbook, an effort is made to standardize the use of the word *product* to encompass all organizations. However, where it can provide greater clarity, the word *service* is occasionally used.

The other word that bears special consideration is *organization*. ISO 9001's diversification has resulted in a proliferation of certifications among nonprofit, educational, and governmental entities. Hence, the generic use of organization is universally applicable. Except in those cases where it clearly makes more sense to use the word *business*, the word *organization* is used.

Finally, one of the great characteristics of organizations is their variety. Products, processes, markets, internal cultures, size, assets, and constraints all contribute to the tableau that is your unique organization. Your QMS must reflect your organization.

It should be reflective of your relationship with your customers and your commitment to fulfilling their requirements. There is no cookie-cutter QMS. ISO 9001:2008 defines the requirements, but it does not dictate the method of application. Utilizing this handbook should allow you to develop or rejuvenate your QMS so that it is a benefit to both you and your customer.

1

ISO 9001 and Small and Medium-Sized Businesses

WHAT IS ISO 9001?

ISO 9001 is an international standard that defines the requirements for establishing a system to manage your organization and processes to better serve your customers.

This standard does not reinvent your company, nor is the process for implementation difficult. It's a logical methodology based on how you run your business. It brings consistency and control to everyday practices. The basic philosophy is: "Do what you say and say what you do!" Further, it augments the effectiveness of processes by providing requirements that help you monitor and analyze key performance indicators for maintenance and improvement.

Over one million organizations around the globe are certified to ISO 9001. The standard has been in place for almost 20 years. Companies utilizing this international standard come from varied fields and industries. Companies as small as one person have been certified.

WHAT DO WE MEAN BY "SMALL AND MEDIUM-SIZED"?

Traditionally, companies with fewer than 50 people are considered small, whereas those with up to 500 employees are considered medium-sized. There is no precise definition, no exact number. For example, an organization can have 90 people, but if 80 of them perform the same routine tasks and top management is encompassed by only two individuals, it might be considered a small business. Conversely, with the advent of virtual technology, a medium- to large-sized software company could easily have fewer than 50 employees. The multiplicity and intricacy of processes, assets, tiers of middle management, use of subcontractors, and complexity of the product also contribute to the determination of "small" versus "medium-sized."

Financial institutions and agencies such as the U.S. Small Business Administration (SBA) have specific criteria for small businesses used to determine financial assistance and loan qualification. This handbook does not adhere to those strict guidelines.

Therefore, depending on the purpose of the categorization, any reasonable definition is correct. Ultimately, the decision is yours. You get to decide if you consider your organization to be small or medium-sized. It is not particularly relevant to the utility of this handbook. Suffice it to say that this handbook has broad applicability.

It's important to keep in mind that smaller organizations do tend to share similar characteristics. They tend to have fewer individuals in top management or middle management. They often have less complicated processes. That, in turn, often means fewer documents. However, that isn't always the case. A small design firm might have many, many documents.

Smaller organizations have fewer people, so there tends to be extensive cross-training. One individual may wear many hats. In organizations with fewer than 20 people, it's more likely that individuals will have multiple tasks. Perhaps the most ubiquitous example is the shipper/receiver. This individual has responsibility for both functions. Yet in an ISO 9001 system, those processes are considered to be separate and unique. Shipping is generally the next sequential process after manufacturing or final inspection. The requirements are found in subclause 7.5.5. Receiving is a process directly related to the purchasing function and more closely associated with subclause 7.4.3. So you have one person and one job description but two distinct processes.

Communication occurs differently in smaller organizations. There's usually only one location and one building. Consequently, communication is generally face to face, and internal e-mails are less frequent. Meetings tend to be less formal, and changes are implemented with minimal bureaucracy. This doesn't absolve the organization from the requirements for well-controlled documentation and record retention. It simply means that it will occur differently than it would in a large corporation where, for example, engineering change notices might need approvals from process owners on three continents.

Implementing a quality management system (QMS) is not easier or harder in a small organization than it is in a large one. Resources are different; each has its own unique challenges, constraints, and advantages. The thing to always bear in mind is that this is your organization and these are your processes.

WHY 9001?

ISO 9001:2008 is the most widely used QMS standard in the world. There's good reason for its success. Simply stated, it works.

There are a variety of reasons for implementing a QMS. Before continuing, it's worth reviewing the value and benefits of your implementation project. The following sections discuss some of the great reasons for establishing and implementing an ISO 9001 QMS.

To Improve the Way the Company Does Business

This is the single best reason for "doing ISO." It will help you improve your organization. It will help by bringing consistency and definition to processes, which will result in fewer defects and more efficient practices. Think of it as an investment. The return on investment (ROI) will pay dividends over time. Better control means decreased errors and fewer resources wasted on redoing, reworking, and repairing. It means improved efficiency and less firefighting. All of these things cost money and are a drain on the bottom line. The implementation of a QMS is an investment in your business, just like a capital expenditure for new equipment or software.

To Fulfill a Customer Requirement

Over the years the number of customers requiring ISO 9001 certification as the minimum criterion for qualification as a supplier has grown dramatically. It makes sense. Any organization's ability to fulfill its customers' requirements is directly relevant to the integrity of its supply chain. Having good suppliers who can provide top-quality product on time consistently and reliably is an indispensable requisite for viability. However, conducting on-site visits, periodic audits, and other qualification activities is a drain on an organization's time and resources. It's much more economical to select a supplier that has been certified by an independent third party (like a registrar) as conforming to the requirements of an international QMS standard—ISO 9001:2008. Considering the growth in global commerce and the costs associated with doing business around the world, choosing to rely on this standard is a smart financial decision.

To Solve Problems

In section 8 of the standard are two important subclauses that can help you anticipate problems through a preventive action process and solve problems so they don't recur using a corrective action process. Both are effective processes that will help you address those problems that are a drain on your financial resources. Over time, you'll discover that consistent utilization of these processes results in fewer catastrophic events that not only affect the bottom line, but also harm your reputation and your relationship with customers.

To Increase Market Share

This benefit comes to you in two different ways. First, your status as an organization that is certified to ISO 9001 is a great marketing tool. A good QMS is something to be proud of. Second, as was already mentioned, the system should save you money over time. That means financial resources will be freed up, allowing you to explore new markets, conduct more research and development projects, and acquire technology that will enhance your ability to serve existing and future customers.

To Minimize Waste, Scrap, and Rework

ISO 9001 is about more than just conformance to a standard. Within its pages are found requirements that augment an organization's ability to monitor processes, analyze performance indicators, set objectives, and take action to improve. In practical terms this means that, properly implemented, your ISO 9001 QMS should help you address many of the issues that affect your efficiency and your cash flow. You end up developing the tools to reduce waste and mitigate the effects of inefficient processes.

To Increase Customer Confidence

Getting selected as a qualified supplier is only the beginning of your relationship with your customers. As mentioned earlier, an ISO 9001 certificate is often the shortcut to becoming an approved supplier. However, maintaining that status and being able to consistently demonstrate your ability to meet and exceed customer requirements is the challenge you face. Your ISO 9001–compliant system will provide you with the structure and processes you will need to ensure your status as the supplier of choice over time. Again, through monitoring of processes, conducting preventive actions, addressing problems robustly, and finding ways to improve, you create the perceptions that increase your customers' confidence in your organization.

To Save Money (or Make More Money)

All of the benefits just mentioned ultimately translate into a healthier bottom line.

A FEW WORDS ABOUT REGISTRARS

Third-party organizations that conduct assessment and grant certification to ISO 9001 are called *registrars*. Internationally, they are often referred to as certification bodies (CBs), and organizations are said to be certified. In the United States we use the terms *registered* and *certified* interchangeably. In order for your organization to be certified, it must be assessed by a registrar.

There are several important things to remember about registrars and the certification process.

This Is Not an Award

Certification is not an award; it's a recognition of conformance to ISO 9001:2008 (or, in some cases, another sector-specific standard). This is not the end of the journey; it's the beginning. If your expectation is that you can undergo the certification assessment, post your certificate on the wall, and then forget about the system, you will eventually lose your certification. You are expected to maintain and improve your system, hence the requirement for periodic surveillance audits.

Selecting a Registrar

There are multiple factors to consider when selecting a registrar. It's important to verify that the registrar is accredited by a recognized body. There are organizations out there that purport to provide certification but have no recognized credentials. Accreditation means your certificate will be recognized both nationally and internationally. It means other registrars and their customers will acknowledge your certificate. If your customers require you to be certified, they're expecting that certificate to come from a reputable organization. The accreditor's logo is always displayed on the certificate along with the registrar's own logo. The absence of an accrediting body's logo is an indication that your certificate will probably not be universally recognized. That means all the money you've invested in the actual assessment (on-site audit, travel expenses, etc.) has been wasted.

When selecting a registrar, ask who their accrediting body is. There are many. A few of the ones more commonly used include ANAB (ANSI-ASQ National Accreditation Board), UKAS (United Kingdom Accreditation Service), and RvA (Rood Voor Accreditatie).

Ensure that the registrar has auditors with expertise in your particular field. If your organization serves the medical device industry, you don't want an auditor whose chief experience is in the petroleum business. Your audit will be a much more valuable process if the auditor understands your business. Less time will be wasted explaining industry practices, and the findings will provide much better opportunities for improvement.

Ask questions and ensure you understand the registrar's procedures and rules for such things as scheduling, the actual assessment process, reporting, actions required for minor or major nonconformances, their appeals process, and any use of their logo on your Web site or literature.

If you already have a registrar and a certified QMS, you should already know the answer to many of these questions. If you don't, ask. If your registrar is reluctant to answer any of your questions, start looking for a new registrar.

Finally, people sometimes wonder why they have to deal with periodic surveillance audits. Certification is not a one-time event. It's a controlled approach to managing your organization to better serve your customers. Things change. You may add a product line or pick up a second shift. You may move to a larger facility or decide to subcontract a major process. Your system needs to be robust enough to manage these changes. The registrar's surveillance visits, as well as your own internal audits, serve to ensure continued compliance even when things are in flux.

GETTING GOING

Regardless of whether this is an entirely new experience for your organization or whether you're trying to improve your current QMS, this handbook should provide you with benefits beyond the actual certification process. In either case, you get to do some spring cleaning. You can brush away cobwebs from old documents, look at processes with fresh eyes, and conduct refresher training to get people back on course.

For those of you just starting out, here are a few tips:

- Buy a copy of the ISO 9001:2008 standard and read it. You don't want to be getting information second- or third-hand about requirements.

- Tell your people what you want to do and why. If you don't want to announce it to the entire organization, at least make sure key personnel have been informed.

- Enlist individuals to manage the project. In a very small organization, this may be one individual. Larger organizations should try to select two or three people (the quality manager plus two process owners with good communication skills). Tell them to familiarize themselves with the standard. The actual requirements (from the introduction to the end of the last clause, excluding annexes) are encompassed in 18 pages. Then, get them to read the relevant parts of this book for direction. Chapters 3–9 provide specific guidance on various aspects of the QMS vis-à-vis your organization.

- Let the people plan the project with your guidance. They should:

  — Assess what documents you currently have

  — Decide what needs to be revised, replaced, or discarded

  — Determine what additional documents will be required

  — Apportion out the writing/editing

  — Estimate the time that will be required for this phase of the project

  — Ensure the inclusion of any additional processes mandated by your customers

- Give your people the time they need to work on the project and reassure them that you will support their work.

The next steps in the project will unfold at a pace proportionate to the amount of time that is being devoted to it. Try not to extend the project unnecessarily. Otherwise, people will lose focus and think of it as a passing fad. Their interest will wane and it will take you even longer to get things well established. But don't rush the project to the point where you've lost the value inherent in the process. You'll need time to conduct audits, initiate corrective actions, revise documents, and do a couple of rounds of training.

The thing to bear in mind is that you have a healthy organization and you've got some very good, well-established practices. Again, this is not about reinventing the organization.

In subsequent chapters, examples will be provided to help you better understand how to conduct your ISO 9001 implementation project in a manner that will be of benefit to your organization and will help you maintain and improve your QMS.

2

Overview of
ISO 9001:2008

ISO 9001:2008 is a generic QMS model. It can be effectively implemented by organizations of any size across multiple and varied disciplines. It creates a level playing field. This enhances the opportunity for smaller organizations to compete because they conform to the same basic requirements as large organizations. Since companies great and small utilize ISO 9001, it's worth getting a bird's eye view of this extraordinary standard that has global requirements with such broad applicability.

Before proceeding with in-depth details of the requirements found in ISO 9001:2008, it's important to consider the document as a whole. This is important for several reasons. First, the document was developed from the perspective of interrelated processes. Everything is connected. In order to fully grasp the interrelations, it's essential to look at it in its totality. The second reason is that the standard is founded on eight quality management principles (QMPs).

The QMPs are not requirements. They can be more aptly likened to guiding stars. A well-implemented and effective QMS will manifest these principles throughout the organization. Consider them as glittering threads that are woven throughout the tapestry of your QMS. They reflect the character of your organization and allow its attributes to shine, not only for your customers, but also for your own people.

Perhaps the two most prominent QMPs in relation to ISO 9001 are customer focus and the process approach. Together these may be considered the hallmark of this standard. However, all of the QMPs are important and warrant a brief review.

The QMPs are listed here in the order in which they are found in ISO 9000:2005 *Quality management systems—Fundamentals and vocabulary*. Additionally, ISO 10014:2006 *Quality management—Guidelines for realizing financial and economic benefits* utilizes the structure of the eight QMPs to demonstrate how a well-maintained QMS can benefit your organization.

THE QUALITY MANAGEMENT PRINCIPLES

Customer Focus

ISO 9001:2008, in its scope, clearly states that the requirements of the standard are intended to facilitate the ". . . ability to consistently provide product that meets customer . . . requirements, and . . . to enhance customer satisfaction through the effective application of the system, including processes for continual improvement of the system and the assurance of conformity to customer and applicable statutory and regulatory requirements." Throughout ISO 9001 you will find language that deals with understanding customer requirements, ensuring your organization can meet those requirements, and developing methods of communicating with customers, monitoring customer feedback, and assessing customer satisfaction. Without customers, nothing happens. So the primary focus must be on the customer. You'll note that the scope clearly indicates that the path to customer satisfaction lies within your QMS.

As a small or medium-sized enterprise, your relationship with your customers may be different from larger organizations. You may have fewer customers, in which case your relationship is predictably more intimate. Since there are fewer middle managers and support staff, the individuals interacting with customers are often the ones responsible for manufacturing the product or providing the service to the customer. This also means that the processes you use, for example, to measure customer satisfaction are markedly different from those used by a large organization. A large organization may use surveys to gauge customers' perceptions of how they're doing. If they have 10,000 customers and they get back a 3% response, they'll have about 300 data points to graph and analyze. If you have 67 customers and you get feedback from 3%, you'll have exactly 2 surveys to review. Graphing the results is obviously not going to yield any worthwhile information. So, in smaller organizations, different methods have to be applied to monitor customer satisfaction. This will be further discussed in Chapter 9.

Leadership

ISO 9001:2008 places the responsibility for the establishment and implementation of the QMS on top management. In fact, in section 5 the text specifically states that management ". . . shall provide evidence of its commitment to the development and implementation of the quality management system."

That commitment goes far beyond the initial decision to implement ISO 9001:2008. It is reflected in the example that is set and in ongoing visible and vocal support. Leadership in the context of a QMS means that top management communicates effectively, ensures adequate resources are made available, and participates in the QMS processes that relate to their own function. Chief among the processes owned by top management is the management review process, which will be discussed in Chapter 6.

As with all other QMPs, guidance on leadership is found throughout the standard, from the establishment and definition of the QMS to its deployment, to identifying objectives and the metrics to monitor them, and through improvement initiatives.

Management cannot abdicate or delegate responsibility for the QMS. The degree to which management is successful is reflected in the next QMP.

Involvement of People

This QMP asserts the importance of people within your organization. Their talent, their knowledge, and their full engagement are essential to your goals. Without them, customer satisfaction is impossible. Management's endorsement of this QMP is another manifestation of leadership, the preceding QMP.

Within ISO 9001:2008, the section most associated with people is section 6, which deals with training and competence. There are other places in the standard where involvement of people is also reflected. There is reference to the need for the effective communication of their role in the QMS and in the fulfillment of customer requirements. There's also the need for people to have access to requisite documentation and the tools they need to complete tasks. To experience the most benefit from individuals' involvement, management must ensure that they have the necessary resources.

Process Approach

With the 2000 version, ISO 9001 introduced the concept of the process approach. It's a wonderfully logical concept that has been unnecessarily mystified. Fundamentally, what it says is that we need a reason to do something (input), we need to do it (process), and there has to be a verifiable product (output) that matches the defined input.

The inputs are found in requirements—the "shalls" that create the reason to do something. There's an often-ignored efficiency to this concept. Basically, if you don't have a requirement, there is no reason to expend resources; therefore, properly defined inputs take on new significance. In a small business, having streamlined requirements that are well defined should lead to less wasted time, labor, and money. This relates directly to your documentation and will be further discussed in Chapter 5.

The activity (or group of activities) is defined as the process. In order to convert inputs into outputs, you need resources, people, and ancillary stuff such as tools, equipment, and an appropriate environment. The activities are conducted in such a way that they fulfill the requirements (inputs).

The output of any process is a product. It should match the input. Let's say that a machine shop has an order for 2500 rods. The requirements are found on a drawing. It specifies that the rods need to be manufactured from 303 stainless and should be 8 inches long ±.010, with a diameter of 4 inches ±.005. Other documentation related to this process could include a brief work instruction for machine setup and an inspection form. The process might be a cutting operation followed by a turning operation. There might also be the need to deburr. The material required is the 303 stainless; the equipment needed might be a lathe with the appropriate cutting tools. The output of this activity should be finished 303 stainless steel rods with dimensions matching the print.

This is a more general definition than the one we traditionally think of when discussing product as something we furnish to a customer. The only real difference is that when we talk about products as they relate to customer-specified requirements, we're referring to the output of the sum of all the processes that were utilized to achieve the desired result for the customer. That leads us to the next QMP.

Systems Approach to Management

When all the processes mesh together properly, you've got a well-integrated QMS. Processes flow from one to the other. The output of one process becomes the input for the next. For example, the output of an order entry process might be a job assignment for a field technician. That job assignment (input) defines the requirements for the field repair process (activity) that will result in a repaired or refurbished device, which is defined as the product (output).

Internally, you can have successive processes that move you from quotations to order entry, to scheduling, to purchasing, to manufacturing, to inspection, to packaging, to shipping. There will also be many support processes, such as training of personnel, calibration of instruments, maintenance of equipment, warehousing, serialization for traceability, and upkeep of the infrastructure. Additionally, there'll be internal audits and processes to monitor key performance indicators, others to identify (and/or quarantine) defective parts along with corrective actions to address the causes of problems, preventive actions to mitigate risk, and miscellaneous activities that will lead to improvement. And then there's the management review process, where decisions are made about all of the above.

In this way, the organization manifests the next QMP.

Continual Improvement

Continual improvement only makes sense if there's a reason to do it. In this sense, it's reflective of the process approach. We don't seek to improve without purpose. That would be silly.

ISO 9001:2008 makes more than a dozen references to continual improvement. What is it that drives continual improvement initiatives? Change.

Things change. For example, your customers might decide they want faster service. Let's say you're a dry cleaning service and currently it takes you four hours to turn around a garment. Your customers would like to see that cut to about two and a half hours. Or, you may have discovered that the competition can provide the same service in half the time. Either way, in order to remain viable, you need to change how you do something—in this case by addressing this particular aspect of your product (the time it takes to dry clean). This will probably require you to also improve some of your internal processes.

Rather than responding to customer requests or market changes, you may decide to initiate continual improvement initiatives that will augment your profitability. You may opt to streamline processes, purchase updated equipment, add to the range of services offered, or simply change the way you do things. Regardless, standing still is not an option. And any continual improvement efforts usually increase your ability to serve your customers.

Continual improvement allows you to remain relevant in your market, responsive to your customers' evolving needs, and viable as a successful enterprise. Knowing what improvements to implement leads us to our next QMP.

Factual Approach to Decision Making

Decisions made within the structure of a QMS are based on verifiable facts. They aren't based on conjecture or opinion. ISO 9001 provides guidance through requirements related to gathering and analyzing data, monitoring and measuring processes and products, and internal auditing.

This again ensures that resources are not wasted. For example, before a decision is made to purchase a new piece of capital equipment, there is usually a calculation of the ROI. To calculate the ROI it's necessary to have information about the costs related to current repairs, machine downtime, and reworks due to equipment malfunctions. Those costs are summarized and weighed against the cost of new equipment.

The same approach is used for just about any decision in your QMS. It goes back to process approach. We need an input—a defined reason. This is how decisions are made relating to multiple processes. Raw material is purchased based on order fulfillment requirements; jobs are scheduled based on customer requirements and availability of resources (for example, material, people, and machine time). Corrective actions are initiated based on the identification of a problem and the assessment of the effects of that problem. In all cases, decisions are based on objective evidence and reliable data.

This brings us to the last QMP.

Mutually Beneficial Supplier Relations

At first blush, this QMP seems to be a bit of an orphan. It doesn't seem to be related to any of the others. It isn't until we reflect on the first QMP, customer focus, that the connection becomes clear. This QMP brings us full circle and illustrates the profound impact that an organization's supply chain has on its capacity to serve its customers. The other thing that becomes apparent is that we are all at one time or another suppliers to some organizations and customers to others. Let's say there's an industrial distributor who sells (among many other things) gear boxes and cutting tools. In expediting delivery of an order, the distributor might discover that the manufacturer was unable to furnish the gear boxes on time because they were themselves awaiting the delivery of some very specialized cutting tools that they had ordered from the same distributor.

This last QMP extends the concept of the systems approach beyond the actual walls of your organization, encompassing external stakeholders who affect your ability to meet your requirements—that is, to serve your customers. The manner in which we interact with our suppliers is extremely relevant to our organization and to our customers. In his book *Out of the Crisis* (MIT Center for Advanced Engineering Study, 1982), Dr. W. Edwards Deming talks at length about the importance of working with your suppliers. His fourth point states: "End the practice of awarding business on the basis of price tag alone" (p. 31).

Within ISO 9001:2008 are requirements that compel organizations to look beyond price when qualifying and selecting suppliers. Clause 7.4 contains requirements dealing with the selection of suppliers. Part of that process may be acquiring information about a supplier's conformance to ISO 9001 or a similar sector-specific QMS standard. Clause 8.4 requires the organization to gather information about supplier performance. This harkens back to another QMP, factual approach to decision making.

When you wrap all the QMPs together, you get a tableau of what an ISO 9001–compliant organization should look like. It should have responsible individuals at the helm, an engaged workforce, and processes and systems that are well controlled and interconnected. It must be able to respond to change and be ever mindful of the role that customers play in its continued success.

What follows is a brief overview of ISO 9001:2008 sections. Each section is the subject of a chapter later in the book, where requirements are discussed in greater detail.

OVERVIEW OF ISO 9001:2008

Section 1: Scope

The first part of this section deals with the purpose of the standard. It affirms that ISO 9001:2008 is focused on meeting customer requirements as well as applicable statutory and regulatory requirements.

The second part recognizes that there are some requirements that may not be applicable to all organizations. When appropriate, it allows organizations to make exclusions. Exclusions may only be taken to requirements found in section 7.

Section 2: Normative Reference

The standard has only one normative reference: ISO 9000:2005, *Quality management systems—Fundamentals and vocabulary*. Its applicability is discussed in Chapter 4.

Section 3: Terms and Definitions

Certain words have specific or special meaning in ISO 9001:2008. One example is the use of the word *review*. In ISO 9000:2005, 3.8.7, the definition of review states: ". . . activity undertaken to determine the suitability, adequacy and effectiveness (3.2.14) of the subject matter to achieve established objectives." So, within the context of ISO 9001, the review of a process means more than just a cursory check. It would involve, for example, the need to assess the effectiveness of the activity.

Terms with particularly significant definitions will be covered in Chapter 4.

Section 4: Quality Management System

The first clause in this section enumerates what needs to be done to establish a QMS. In general terms it mentions the need to determine what processes are needed, define their sequence, ensure proper control, provide adequate resources, plan, establish appropriate metrics, and implement actions for continual improvement. You'll probably notice that you're already doing some of the things that are mentioned. It bears repeating: This is not about reinventing your company. This is the beginning of creating the virtual infrastructure into which you'll organize and manage many of the things that are already in place. You are simply redefining and refining them within the architecture of a QMS.

The second clause in this section deals with documentation. As we'll see in Chapter 5, there are many different kinds of documents that organizations use. The single most important thing to remember is that regardless of the nature of the documents, there's a need for appropriate control. Documentation includes records.

Section 5: Management Responsibility

The title says it all. This whole section deals with role that management plays in the establishment and maintenance of the QMS. It reiterates the need for customer focus, and it deals with the purpose of the organization, its quality policy, the establishment of quality objectives, defining authority and responsibility, and communicating all of these effectively to people in the organization.

Within the language of section 5 are found the requirements for management review. This process, more than any other, belongs to top management. Chapter 6 elaborates on how small businesses can implement a management review process that creates genuine value.

Section 6: Resource Management

Section 6 covers three different types of resources. The first of these is without a doubt the most important: the human resource. While this is often considered to be the training clause, the requirements actually encompass more than just training. Competence and awareness are also included. Contrary to expectation, in a small business, approaching the requirement of this clause properly should result in less paperwork, not more. This concept is covered in Chapter 7.

The second resource type is the infrastructure. This can include such things as buildings, equipment, vehicles, servers, and telecommunications. This is one of the first areas in ISO 9001:2008 where there will be enormous variation in application. For example, one organization may have a small storefront base from which it operates and 15 specialized vehicles that perform on-site installations. Another company may have five or six buildings with lots of production equipment but no vehicles, since they rely exclusively on common carriers to deliver product to their customers. The manner in which each organization would apply the requirements of this clause would be markedly different.

The final category of resources relates to the work environment. This goes beyond the simple notion of buildings mentioned in the previous category. Work environment may involve factors such as temperature and cleanliness but can also include a myriad of other factors relevant to unique and different industries. These factors are also addressed in Chapter 7.

Section 7: Product Realization

I often tell clients this is where the rubber meets the road. These are the requirements in ISO 9001:2008 that you generally associate with your organization. They comprise the activities that create the visible and tangible manifestation of how you serve your customers. This is the stuff everyone normally does every day.

This is a lengthy section that stretches from planning the major processes you'll need to produce a product all the way through to actual delivery and, in some cases, post-delivery activities. It is the only section in which you may make allowable exclusions. This is reflective of the fact that products and processes differ significantly among various industries, so not all requirements will always be relevant or applicable. There is further discussion of allowable exclusions in Chapter 4.

This section covers quotations, order processing, purchasing, design, manufacturing (or other processes used to produce products—including services), identification and traceability, storage, handling of customer-owned material, shipping, control of measuring and test equipment, and any after-market activities. All of these topics are covered in Chapter 8.

Section 8: Measurement, Analysis, and Improvement

Within this section you'll find the requirements that help you determine how you're doing, what needs to be fixed, what needs to change, what you need to improve, and what's working so well that it needs to be amplified and expanded.

The section begins with assessing customer satisfaction, punctuating once again that the focal point of ISO 9001:2008 is the customer. This is followed by internal auditing. In Chapter 9 there is specific discussion on how to implement an internal auditing process in a small company.

The next clauses in this section deal with monitoring and measuring both processes and product, after which there's a discussion of how to handle nonconforming product (defects and things that do not meet specifications). This is followed by requirements relating to gathering and analyzing data. Again, this is one of the requirements that is often daunting for smaller organizations. Chapter 9 provides tips on fulfilling this requirement in such a manner as to experience real value.

The last clause deals with continual improvement and includes the requirements for both corrective action and preventive action. When properly implemented, these last two processes can result in surprising benefits for the entire organization.

This last clause brings things full circle. Chapter 3 discusses the model of a process-based QMS. It illustrates the placement of monitoring and measuring as the last step before reverting to management responsibility, where decisions are made about how to proceed based on data that has been gathered and analyzed.

That's the overview of ISO 9001:2008. The next chapters explain the requirements in greater detail and provide examples of how to implement your QMS efficiently and effectively.

3

ISO 9001:2008 Introduction

People tend to skip over the introduction to this standard. They probably ignore the introduction to many books they read because, quite frankly, a lot of times the introduction really doesn't have any influence on what you'll read in the rest of the book. That's not the case with ISO 9001:2008.

There's some pretty important stuff in the introduction to ISO 9001:2008 that has direct relevance to your understanding of how to implement it effectively and in conformance to all the requirements. A good comprehension of what's covered in the introduction can also save you time and money and enhance the efficiency and effectiveness of your QMS.

Following is the essential information from the introduction, distilled and presented with a particular slant toward small and medium-sized industries.

0.1 GENERAL

This first part of the introduction gives basic information on the implementation of a QMS and the factors that influence how the requirements of the standard are applied. This is good news for small organizations because it clearly directs that the manner in which you establish your QMS should be based on such things as the environment in which you operate, risks associated with the environment, your products, your processes, and the size and structure of your organization. It goes on to say that the intent is not to imply that all systems or their documentation are uniform. On the contrary, your documentation should reflect your organization. Your QMS and your documentation will be different from those of other organizations, and that's okay.

The other important bit of information gleaned from 0.1 is that anything marked "Note" is provided solely as guidance to understanding and is not a requirement. The technical experts recognized that some requirements might seem ambiguous or less easy to comprehend in some industries. This is particularly true in small organizations that don't have complex systems. The note in 8.2.1 is a great example. It enumerates multiple examples of how customer perception can be monitored. In Chapter 2, it was mentioned that smaller organizations may not benefit from conducting customer surveys. The 8.2.1 note suggests alternate options, relieving small organizations from the onus of creating surveys that provide little value. Conversely, the note in 7.5.3 about configuration management is only something to consider if it applies to your organization. It is not a requirement. Distinguishing notes as guidance could ultimately save you from wasting time and money on nonexistent requirements.

Finally, 0.1 is the first time the phrase *statutory and regulatory requirements* is used. Since this phrase shows up throughout the standard, it's best to deal with it from the onset. ISO 9001:2008 requires an organization to ensure that the statutes and regulations associated with a product are not violated, particularly by omission. ISO 9001:2008 is focused on customer requirements. However, a customer's failure to specify an attribute that is governed by statutory or regulatory requirements does not absolve the organization from the need to conform. For example, a customer could order children's sippy cups with pictures of lions and tigers and giraffes. Even though the customer does not specify that the images need to be applied with lead-free paint, the supplier must consider this as part of the specification for the sippy cup. It's the law. If there are features of your product that come under statutory and regulatory requirements, there has to be evidence that you've ensured conformance. This shows up in several places, most notably in 7.2 Customer-related processes and 7.3 Design and development.

0.2 PROCESS APPROACH

We discussed process approach as a QMP in Chapter 2. The placement of the text in the introduction emphasizes the need for your QMS to be developed, implemented, and maintained using the process approach. Your ISO 9001–compliant system will not work without it, so it's important for everyone involved to understand the concept.

To facilitate that understanding, the technical writers introduced the "Model of a process-based quality management system" in the introduction. It applies the PDCA (plan-do-check-act) model and illustrates its relationship to the fulfillment of customer requirements with the ultimate goal of achieving customer satisfaction. The PDCA steps mirror sections 5–8.

Management plans all the activities that will lead to the fulfillment of customer requirements, including the allocation of resources (Plan). Then processes are implemented (Do). Next, monitoring and measurement are conducted to ensure that processes are working effectively and that product conforms to requirements (Check). Finally, management, through processes such as management review, takes action based on the results (Act) and the cycle begins again. Some of the actions taken will probably result in continual improvement. The illustration in the introduction shows inputs from the customer on one side of this cycle, with the output—which should lead to customer satisfaction—on the other. Therefore, the entire QMS must adhere to the process approach in order to conform to its purpose as well as the stated purpose of ISO 9001:2008, as expressed in the scope.

As we've seen in Chapter 2, adopting the process approach is not an onerous task. On the contrary, it facilitates a logical approach to defining and controlling activities within a structure without needlessly overburdening the system.

0.3 RELATIONSHIP TO ISO 9004

ISO 9001 and ISO 9004 have been called the consistent pair. While ISO 9001 is a requirements standard that is focused on meeting customer requirements, ISO 9004 is a guidance document that addresses the sustainable success of an organization. What this means is that ISO 9004 provides guidance on how to improve, adapt to change, and remain a viable entity in your market. This in turn means that you'll be able to serve your customers, not only now, but in the future—which brings us to the purpose of ISO 9001.

This handbook deals with ISO 9001. However, it's worth mentioning ISO 9004 and the benefits it can offer you. First, it's important to clarify that ISO 9004 is *not* a how-to guide for ISO 9001. Rather, it functions as a road map, with guidance on how to:

- Conduct self-assessments of your organization to identify strengths and weaknesses

- Define your organizational environment and the interested parties who affect your continued ability for sustainable success (these may evolve over time)

- Manage resources

- Establish organizational strategy

- Plan, implement, and monitor processes

- Learn, innovate, and improve

ISO 9004 elaborates on the great structure of ISO 9001 and allows you to amplify the things that are working in order to move beyond simple conformance to a system that has sustained value. The hallmark of ISO 9004 is the concept of periodic self-assessment and awareness of the changes both within and outside of your company that make it possible for you to address the needs of customers and stakeholders (interested parties). It helps you to remain flexible and responsive so that you can experience benefit from the continual improvements you undertake.

While it is a tremendous resource, you do not need to use ISO 9004 in order to have an ISO 9001–compliant QMS.

0.4 COMPATIBILITY WITH OTHER MANAGEMENT SYSTEMS

There is an array of other quality management systems. Some organizations are required to conform to more than one. Examples include:

- ISO 14001 *Environmental management systems— Requirements with guidance for use*

- ISO/TS 16949 *Quality management systems—Particular requirements for application of ISO 9001:2008 for automotive production and relevant service part organizations*

- ISO 13485 *Medical devices—Quality management systems—Requirements for regulatory purposes*

- AS9100 *Quality management systems—Requirements for aviation, space, and defense organizations*

- ISO 17025 *General requirements for the competence of testing and calibration laboratories*

Many of these standards are based on ISO 9001. Others have been developed with the deliberate intention of ensuring alignment with ISO 9001. The structure often mirrors ISO 9001, with the addition of extra requirements. For example, AS9100 which deals with aviation, space, and defense industries, has an additional requirement under 4.2.4 relating to records held by suppliers. That requirement does not conflict with ISO 9001. It simply means that in addition to the requirements found in ISO 9001, the organization must add one "shall" in order to conform to AS9100. This can be done in one of two ways:

1. The organization can apply the requirement dealing with records held by suppliers for aviation customers to all its supplier records, creating one uniform system. This might simplify the documented records procedure and avoid confusion. However, if there are multiple methods of handling the records that would result in a cumbersome and expensive process, the organization might opt for the second method.

2. The organization can instead define in its documented records procedure which specific supplier-held records must be handled in a special way for aviation customers and go on to state that all other such records for other customers are handled in a different way.

In either case, the organization is in conformance with the requirements of both QMS standards. This is the case with most requirements. In some cases, sector-specific requirements can help to improve your ISO 9001–based QMS. Indeed, this handbook can in many instances be as useful to organizations that have chosen to implement a sector-specific QMS instead of ISO 9001.

Ultimately, conformance to ISO 9001 complements other management system models and in most instances will facilitate their integration into your organization's QMS.

4

ISO 9001:2008
Sections 1, 2, and 3

With this chapter, we begin a more detailed discussion of the application of ISO 9001:2008. As with the introduction, the first three sections are often glossed over, but they contain information that is important to an organization's ability to implement an effective QMS that conforms to the requirements of ISO 9001:2008.

SECTION 1: SCOPE

Under the general requirements is the need to have a system that demonstrates the organization's consistent ability to provide product that meets customer requirements as well as statutory and regulatory requirements. I think this is one of the great examples of the value of this standard to small businesses.

The chief concern that many customers have when dealing with smaller organizations is that their relative size will adversely affect their ability to provide product consistently. They worry that smaller enterprises will be less likely to maintain the robust processes and manage the resources that allow them to be a reliable supplier. ISO 9001:2008 is designed to allay those fears. Whatever its size, an organization that conforms to ISO 9001 requirements has a system that fosters consistent fulfillment of customer requirements. An organization does not have to be big and complex to be an effective contributor to its customers' supply chains.

As a small or medium-sized enterprise, you have two mandates within the scope: to provide product that conforms to customer, statutory, and regulatory requirements, and to provide the product within the structure of a QMS that allows you to demonstrate your ability to do this consistently.

The second part of section 1 deals with application of the standard. It basically says that ISO 9001:2008 is a generic standard that applies to organizations regardless of size or type of product offering. It goes on to state that when a requirement does not apply to an organization, the organization can claim an exclusion. What this means is that you may determine that certain activities do not occur within your organization. Exclusions may only be taken under section 7. This is actually quite reasonable since the other sections deal with requirements that are common to all organizations: the need to establish a documented system (section 4), the need for top management to assume responsibility (section 5), the need for resources (section 6), and the need to monitor and measure products and processes (section 8).

The only section where there is the potential that a requirement might not be applicable, therefore, is section 7. Following are examples of exclusions that may be taken.

7.3: Design and Development

This exclusion is fairly common with job shops, assembly houses, and subcontractors. In each instance, the organization has no design responsibility. The drawings, specifications, and other product-related requirements are developed entirely by the customer and provided to the organization. Machine shops regularly fabricate parts to customers' prints; an electronic assembly house uses a customer's prints or Gerber data and bills of materials to populate printed circuit boards.

Let's say instead that the product is a delivery service. The supplier picks up the customer's package and delivers it to a specified location. The delivery company may select the route it will travel, but it does not design the roads. An exclusion in this case would be justified.

In both of these instances, there is the possibility that the design requirement would be applicable. Taking another look at the electronic assembly house example, let's assume that the customer has provided general specifications but has asked the supplier to develop the Gerber data, which are used to lay out the components on the board. In that case, the organization would be involved in design activities and an exclusion would not be appropriate. Similarly, if the delivery service has a regular guaranteed route for a customer with predesignated stops that takes into consideration factors like perishable goods, prioritized packages, and peak travel times, an argument might be made that the design of the route is part of the product.

7.5.3: Identification and Traceability

This is an interesting requirement in terms of exclusions because it's possible to be required to conform to the first part but not the second. Identification is a standard practice in most organizations. Either the product is identified in a manufacturing environment or the documentation that accompanies the service is identified in a service environment.

However, in some cases there is no need for traceability. For example, the nails used in a widget are generic, mass-produced parts having little effect on its function. They are purchased by the millions and the supplier has an automatic replenishment program. Traceability is not needed, nor is it achievable without developing an elaborate system that would double the price of a commodity that has a short shelf life and carries no risk to the user. The customer doesn't need it and it is irrelevant to the product specification. In this case, an exclusion is a wise, cost-saving decision.

7.5.4: Customer Property

This is also a very common exclusion. Very simply, if you don't use customer-owned material in the production of the product, you can claim an exclusion.

There's a note in this subclause that should be carefully heeded when considering this exclusion. It states that intellectual property or personal data can be included under this heading. If, for example, you have a small company that handles medical billing, all of the patients' information is considered customer property, and you cannot, therefore, claim an exclusion.

The other thing that is often missed with this clause is non-warranty repairs and refurbishing. Your organization may generate a certain amount of revenue from the servicing of products whose warranties have expired. This service (the output of your processes) constitutes a product. The customer sends the product back. You evaluate it and quote an estimated cost to repair. The product that you provide to the customer is a repaired/refurbished device. Therefore, the customer has provided you their property to be incorporated into the finished "product." In these instances, the requirements of 7.5.4 apply, and an exclusion may not be claimed.

Conversely, you could decide to totally exclude the repair portion of your business from the scope of your QMS. In that case, the defined scope would make it clear that repair isn't part of the organization's QMS. What that would mean is that none of those processes would be considered certified under your ISO 9001–compliant system. While this might be a good financial decision, there are some industries, particularly those with regulatory impact like aviation or medical devices, that might not look favorably on a certificate of limited scope.

There are some much more obvious reasons for excluding certain processes. Years ago the owner of a chemical whole-sale operation related to me how they had taken on a contract to bag dog food during a downturn in the economy so that

Table 4.1 Evidence for justification of exclusion.

Exclusion	Product	Evidence
7.3 Design and development	Machined steel parts	Customer's drawings and documents describing the manufacturing process
7.5.3 Traceability	Widgets	Drawing demonstrating generic specification for nails and fasteners
7.5.4 Customer property	Printed circuit board	Bills of material and/or purchase orders showing that all components for product are purchased

they wouldn't have to lay anyone off. It kept all their people employed for about nine months, until the regular business picked up again. The dog food bagging processes obviously would not have been within the scope of their QMS.

Finally, exclusions must be justified. There must be a verifiable method of proving that the requirement does not apply to your organization. In most cases, proving a justified exclusion is not too difficult. Table 4.1 lists some tips for providing evidence of justification of an exclusion.

The only other thing to bear in mind is that an exclusion is not the same as an outsourced process. An exclusion is something that simply doesn't apply to your organization. An outsourced process is one that does apply but that is carried out by an organization that is external to your organization. Outsourced processes are discussed in the next chapter.

SECTION 2: NORMATIVE REFERENCE

The standard has only one normative reference: ISO 9000:2005, *Quality management systems—Fundamentals and vocabulary*. Basically, what this means is that terms and concepts that are contained in ISO 9000 create the foundation for ISO 9001, and their definitions, by extension, are implicit in the application and implementation of ISO 9001. As was mentioned in previous chapters, the QMPs are relevant to the effectiveness of ISO 9001. The best example is the process approach, which is explained in the introduction of ISO 9001 and is essential to the implementation of your QMS.

SECTION 3: TERMS AND DEFINITIONS

Section 3 also refers to ISO 9000. In this case, it focuses on terms and definitions. Some words have specific meanings within a QMS that may be either broader or narrower than those found in a standard dictionary. We've already covered the use of the word *product*.

Table 4.2 lists some of the more commonly used terms along with their definitions as found in ISO 9000:2005. Understanding how these terms are used in ISO 9001 could increase applicability and decrease the likelihood of misinterpreting a requirement. This is just a brief list; acquiring a copy of ISO 9000:2005 is advisable.

Table 4.2 Commonly used terms and definitions from ISO 9000:2005.

Term	Definition	Comment
Correction	Action taken to eliminate a detected nonconformity	Understanding the difference between this and corrective action can save both time and money. See Chapter 9.
Corrective action	Action to eliminate the cause of a detected nonconformity or other undesirable situation	It's important to remember that this process is focused on the cause of the problem. See Chapter 9.

(Continued)

Table 4.2   Commonly used terms and definitions from ISO 9000:2005. (Continued)

Term	Definition	Comment
Defect	Non-fulfillment of a requirement related to an intended use or specified use	Note that defects are more closely related to the product, whereas *nonconformity* (see below) has a broader definition.
Document	Information and its supporting medium	This definition makes it clear that you have great latitude in deciding how you will document requirements. See Chapter 5.
Nonconformity	Non-fulfillment of a requirement	It's important to realize that nonconformities aren't just related to a quality standard. They're relevant to requirements found in work instructions, customer specifications, and many other documents.
Preventive action	Action to eliminate the cause of a potential nonconformity or other undesirable potential situation	This process deals with risk. Understanding how to implement this requirement in a small organization is covered in Chapter 9.
Procedure	Specified way to carry out an activity or a process	Notice that this definition doesn't mention documentation. Some procedures are not documented. Others are defined in things like work instructions, production routers, etc. This is covered in Chapter 5.

(Continued)

Table 4.2 Commonly used terms and definitions from ISO 9000:2005. (Continued)

Term	Definition	Comment
Process	Set of interrelated or interacting activities which transforms inputs into outputs	Process approach means that all activities mirror this definition of inputs and outputs.
Record	Document stating results achieved or providing evidence of activities performed	Records come in all shapes and sizes— another example of the many choices you have in establishing your QMS.
Review	Activity undertaken to determine the suitability, adequacy, and effectiveness of the subject matter to achieve established objectives	This definition is particularly relevant because it includes determining adequacy and effectiveness. Whenever the standard mentions *review*, it includes those concepts.
Top management	Person or group of people who directs and controls an organization at the highest level	It's important to identify top management in your organization since there are certain requirements that are the specific responsibility of this individual (or group of individuals).

5

ISO 9001:2008
Section 4

There are three basic concepts covered in section 4 of the standard. The first clause covers two of them: the general requirements for your QMS and the requirements surrounding outsourced processes. The second clause covers documentation. The flow is logical. You begin by identifying what your QMS will look like, and then you follow through with the documents that will define that which you have identified.

4.1 GENERAL REQUIREMENTS

Clause 4.1 establishes the requirements for your QMS in broad strokes. It requires you to identify your processes, determine their sequence and interactions, establish the criteria for ensuring effective control, ensure the availability of adequate resources, define methods for monitoring and measuring products and processes, and have the ability to take action to improve. It's beneficial at this point to remember that an ISO 9001 implementation isn't about reinventing your organization. The mantra is: "Do what you say. Say what you do." Clause 4.1 helps you begin the process of saying what you do.

Two things should become apparent as you move through this process. First, you're already doing many of things that are required by the standard—purchasing, design, production, inspection, training, and so forth. You are bringing standard definition and control to that which already exists. The second thing that will become evident is that the concept of process approach is going to be very helpful in putting your QMS together, if you bear in mind that the output of one activity is often the input to the next one.

What follows are tips on how to begin.

Step 1

Identify your major processes. If you have a lot of activities, try doing this as a brainstorming session with two or three process owners.

Step 2

Once you've got all the processes listed, sort them into groups. They'll fall into three predictable categories: processes directly related to making product (what ISO 9001 calls "product realization"), ancillary processes that support the product realization processes, and management system processes that control the activities that help you manage the entire system. This last category doesn't necessarily mean that these processes are owned by the quality department or management. It just means that they permeate the entire QMS, so all process owners have some level of accountability for their effective implementation.

Table 5.1 provides an example of how an initial categorization of processes (or activities) might look in a small industrial distributorship.

Looking at this table we can see that not everything is an actual process. Some are just activities; some are subsets within processes. For example, cycle counting is an activity within the warehouse management process. When you get ready to create documents defining that process, cycle counting may end up being a section within that document. Or, in some cases, an activity may warrant a brief work instruction or guidance document. Not everything on the list requires a documented proce-

Table 5.1 First-round brainstorming of processes.

Product realization processes	Support processes	QMS processes
• Quotations • Order picking • Purchasing • Receiving • Order processing • Expediting • Cycle counting • Warehouse management • Stocking • Handling returns • Inspection • Private labeling • Sending out for plating • Packaging • Shipping	• Training • Calibrating scales • Catalog maintenance • Filing	• Issuing credit • Maintaining procedures • Handling customer complaints • Doing vendor returns • Issuing RMAs (return material authorizations) to customers

dure, as we'll see in the second part of this chapter. However, having this list will help you decide what processes you want to document and what format the documents might take. Continuing with the example of an industrial distributor, we've decided that quotations and order processing might be combined into one procedure. Inspection requirements could be a section in three different procedures: one dealing with receiving materials, one for any in-process value-added activities like labeling or painting, and one for checking before product ships out.

This exercise also helps you identify any exclusions that you may claim. For example, if you are a distributor that generally drop-ships material to customers—in which case the product never passes through your facility—then incoming inspection is not one of your processes and you'll be able to claim an exclusion to 7.4.3.

In Table 5.1, there's at least one activity that is an outsourced process: sending parts out for plating. This will be discussed further on in this chapter. For the moment, it's important to make sure any outsourced processes get identified within your QMS.

Finally, other things will occur to you as you look at the list and compare it against ISO 9001:2008 requirements. Some things aren't in the right column. Both filing and catalog maintenance are really activities under document and record management. And there are some elements that are missing. In this case we need to add corrective action, preventive action, internal audits, management review, and data analysis to the last column. This takes us to the next step.

Step 3

Add the missing processes and any others you may have thought of in the interim. Identify things that are really activities within other processes. And, finally, put the processes in the first column in the order in which they generally occur. The other two columns will not be so easily sequenced since they support everything in the first column at varying times. Table 5.2 illustrates this step.

By the time you've finished this exercise, you will have fulfilled the requirements of 4.1 and will be on your way to meeting the requirements of 4.2. As we'll see later on, one of the requirements for your quality manual is that you identify your processes and the interaction among them.

There's nothing magical about the outcome of this exercise. Nor is there a requirement that you organize your processes as described. The intent with this exercise is to give you some easy tips to help you bring structure to your QMS and its documentation.

Step 4

In this next step, you can take the sequenced processes and put them into one or two very basic flowcharts. If you have few processes, you can skip over this step.

Table 5.2   Organization of processes.

Product realization processes	Support processes	QMS processes
• Quotations • Order processing • Purchasing —Expediting • Receiving —Inspection • Order picking —Sending out for plating —Private labeling • Warehouse management —Stocking —Cycle counting —Handling returns • Packaging —Shipping	• Training • Calibration • Warehouse maintenance	• Maintaining documents and records —Filing —Catalog maintenance —IT/IMS (information management system) • Handling customer complaints —Issuing RMAs (return material authorizations) to customers —Issuing credit —Doing vendor returns • Internal audits • Corrective action • Preventive action • Management review • Data analysis

Figure 5.1 is arranged to illustrate the product realization processes, showing the sequences and some of the interactions. Along the left are some of the support processes. Bearing in mind that this is only an example, you can see that the organization (in this case a distributor) has linked training to processes where the absence of training might affect the ability to meet customer requirements or result in errors. The calibration process supports the inspection process by ensuring that the equipment used is properly controlled. Warehouse maintenance, addressing the infrastructure requirements of ISO 9001,

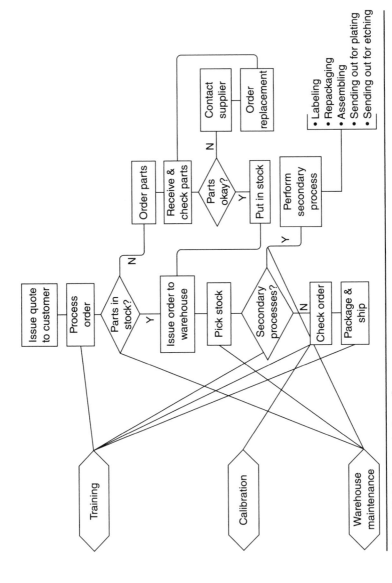

Figure 5.1 Interrelation of processes.

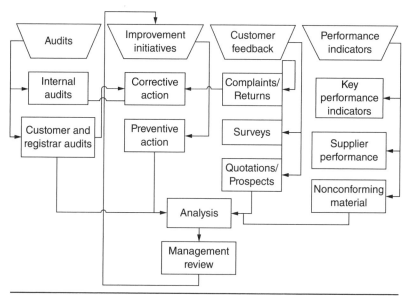

Figure 5.2 QMS processes.

is linked to processes relating to stocking and protecting product. Finally, note that there is a small insert on the right to allow for the inclusion of outsourced processes when needed (labeling, repackaging, etc.).

This is a high-level chart and does not include details. There is no requirement for any specified method of documenting sequence and interaction. How you decide to illustrate your processes, the level of detail, and how many charts you ultimately use is your decision.

Figure 5.2 shows the QMS processes. It shows some very important interrelations among such things as internal audits, corrective actions, and improvements. It also illustrates that everything should ultimately flow back to management for review, bringing things full circle.

The next thing ISO 9001:2008 mentions are outsourced processes. These are processes that are required in order for your QMS to be complete (and to meet customer requirements) but that are carried out by organizations or other parties that are external to your organization. Organizations outsource processes for one of two reasons: Either they lack the resources or expertise to conduct the process, or they choose not to conduct the process in-house for financial, scheduling, or efficiency reasons. Outsourced processes are *not* exclusions. Here are two examples to illustrate the difference.

An assembly shop gets all the design information from their customer to build a product. The assembly shop may take an exclusion because it has no responsibility for the design. Another assembly house has a customer that gives them general specifications and then contracts with them to design and manufacture a product. The assembly house, having no on-site engineering staff, subcontracts the design portion of the contract to a design firm. The assembly house does have responsibility for the design in this case because the design is part of the product specified in the contract with the customer. The assembly house, therefore, may not claim an exclusion to the design clause of ISO 9001. Note that the language concerning outsourced processes is in section 4—not in section 7. This placement is deliberate in order to prevent organizations from inadvertently claiming exclusions and abdicating responsibility for important processes.

Following is a list of examples of typical outsourced processes:

- Heat treat/plating/painting

- Field service

- Remote warehousing

- Independent testing/validation

- Development of user manuals

- Entire manufacturing process

- Off-site record storage

- Marketing/surveys

- Call centers

This list is not all-inclusive. Any process that is a part of your QMS that is performed by someone from outside is considered outsourced. This includes processes that are carried out by a sister division or at the corporate level.

Here's what you need to remember about outsourced processes: You have to describe how they fit into your QMS. If you review Figure 5.1, you'll note that the outsourced processes are identified and that the chart illustrates in general terms how they fit in. Any documents relating to your processes need to have some text referencing the outsourced processes. For example, say a distributor has a work instruction for order fulfillment. In the document, there's a section that describes what happens when customers need to have parts plated. It could read:

> When the pick list is generated, parts needing to be plated are listed on a separate packing slip that is used to ship the parts to the plating house with a purchase order. The rest of the order is segregated. After the parts are retuned and verified, the information is transferred onto the pick list and the parts are added to the rest of the order.

ISO 9001:2008 states that the level of control for outsourced processes is dependent on their potential impact on your ability to meet customer requirements. In this example there would also have to be some evidence of how the supplier was qualified and what the acceptance criteria were for the parts. Let's say your organization has a customer that requires you to maintain copies of all pertinent records at a remote third-party facility. The level of control may simply be ensuring that the facility is a reputable, dependable data storage provider. You should have records showing that you've verified their credentials.

Other processes may be more complicated. Let's say your organization is outsourcing a group of manufacturing processes that are critical to your product. In that case, your level of control would include several, if not all, of the following:

- Supplier audit

- Development of detailed manufacturing drawings and build instructions

- On-site training of their staff

- Periodic visits to assess their process control

- An individual from your organization working at their facility

Sometimes people say to me that they have no control over a plating application or a heat-treater. They just send the parts out and then get them back. Again, it's important to stress that turning a process over to a third party does not absolve the organization from responsibility for the output of the process. When working with organizations like platers and heat-treaters it is possible to conduct audits, to verify conformance to their own industry requirements, and to require reports and/or test results that confirm the fulfillment of your order to your specifications. AIAG (Automotive Industry Action Group), for example, has developed documents that facilitate the auditing of processes that are often outsourced, such as plating and heat-treating.

The other thing to consider is, again, criticality. Parts that are being sent out for a secondary process will probably have hours or days of labor invested in them. While the provider of the outsourced process may compensate your organization if there's a loss, the likelihood is that you won't recoup lost rework time or that you'll be late fulfilling your customer's order. Additionally, if customer-owned material is incorporated into the product that is sent out to a third party, your organization incurs the liability for the customer's property.

A site visit or research to confirm conformance to industry standards is a wise investment with many outsourced processes.

In short, if you're subcontracting a process to an outside organization, you have an outsourced process. You need to identify that fact in your documentation and describe how you handle the arrangement, bearing in mind that controls should be proportionate to the importance of the process relative to your ability to serve your customer.

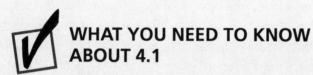

WHAT YOU NEED TO KNOW ABOUT 4.1

You must:

- Identify your processes

- Define the sequence of processes

- Describe the interaction of processes

- Ensure that outsourced processes are included

- Ensure that the method of control of outsourced processes is proportionate to their criticality

4.2 DOCUMENTATION REQUIREMENTS

There are three things covered in this clause: the quality manual, document control, and control of records. You can save a lot of time over the years by spending a little more time up front developing your document control system properly. This is the first of six times ISO 9001 states that you must have a documented procedure. This will be discussed later in the chapter.

You get to decide how your documentation system will work. You already have many documents that your organization uses successfully. You should be able to incorporate most, if not all, into your QMS. Identify the documents that you have and assess them. Some will be fine as they are, while others may require revision to conform to the requirements of ISO 9001:2008.

You are required to have a quality manual. It does not have to be long or detailed. In actuality, it sets out the purpose of your organization in broad terms and should, therefore, be concise. ISO 9001:2008 has only three requirements for your quality manual:

- A definition of the scope of your organization, which includes any justified exclusions. A medical test lab might describe its scope as the analysis of medical specimens and reporting of results to medical providers. It would take an exclusion to the requirements of 7.3 because it has no design responsibilities. A short narrative about the organization is a nice marketing tool, since many customers often request a copy of the quality manual. It's not a bad idea—but it's not a requirement.

- Documented procedures that have been established or reference to them. This is generally handled by referring to a master document list that contains a listing of all the documents that the organization uses. If an organization has only a few documented procedures, it may choose to list them right in the quality manual.

- A description of the interaction between processes in the QMS. The flowcharts that appeared earlier in this chapter fulfill this requirement easily. They not only create a nice pictorial representation of your operation but also illustrate how well your processes flow.

We shouldn't minimize the significance of a quality manual. It is often referred to as the organization's top-level document. It articulates what your organization is all about. You get to decide what it looks like and how elaborate it is. However, the only requirements imposed by ISO 9001 on your quality manual are those that were just mentioned.

Most organizations structure their documents using a tiered method that's fairly standard across many industries. The document structure resembles a pyramid (see Figure 5.3). There's no requirement that your documents conform to this kind of structure. However, the tiered approach does help to organize and manage documentation. Each category of documents flows from the one above it. The lower-tiered documents tend to be more detailed and specific to a process or product.

A machine shop could have seven or eight procedures but have no work instruction, utilizing a combination of routers (production travelers), drawings, and specifications to manufacture a product. A test lab could have a dozen procedures and a library of test methods procured from an industry service. These test methods are referred to as *documents of external origin* and will be discussed later in this chapter.

ISO 9001:2008 requires you to have adequate documentation to define and control the processes. With six notable exceptions, it leaves the format and structure of these documents to your determination.

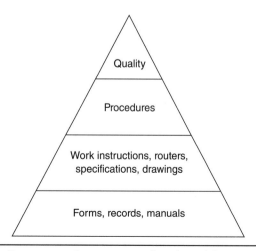

Figure 5.3   Documentation structure tiered model.

Let's deal with the exceptions. In six different spots, the standard requires you to have a "documented procedure." If you look back to the definitions in Chapter 4, a procedure is defined as a "specified way to carry out an activity or a process." It does not necessarily require it to be documented. However, throughout most industries, when the term *procedure* is used, it often implies a documented procedure. The term *procedure,* when used in the rest of this text, will refer to a documented procedure.

The six places where ISO 9001 specifically requires a procedure to be documented are:

- 4.2.3 Control of documents

- 4.2.4 Control of records

- 8.2.2 Internal audit

- 8.3 Control of nonconforming product

- 8.5.2 Corrective action

- 8.5.3 Preventive action

This does not mean these are the only documents you need. The standard clearly states that it requires an organization to have "documents, including records, determined by the organization to be necessary to ensure the effective planning, operation, and control of its processes."

The documents can come in many formats and media. They can be hard copy or electronic, video or some other less conventional media for containing requirements. Some formats might include illustrated manuals, photos, known-good samples, posters, schedules, training videos, bulleted lists, or forms—to name just a few. For example, you may have a form that is used as a checklist when repairing a customer's product. The form contains all the requirements for verification of the product so you do not necessarily need a work instruction describing what needs to be checked. When you've completed the field replacement, the completed checklist becomes the record providing evidence that the process was completed and the product was acceptable.

You have many documents that define requirements. Organizing them will minimize redundancies and significantly decrease the amount of new documents you'll need to create for your QMS. Here is a brief list of the many documents you may already have:

Quality manual

Procedures

Work instructions

Drawings

Spec sheets

Machinery programs

Process maps

Training materials

Web site

Operating manual

Job aids

Contracts

Travelers/Routers

Brochures

Package inserts

Industry regulations

Schedules

ISO 9001:2008 has the following requirements for your documentation.

Documents Must Be Approved Before Being Issued

The approval needs to be apparent or at least verifiable. Documents should have either a real or virtual (electronic) signature.

Alternately, some documents are considered approved by the manner in which they are issued. For example, in a manufacturing environment, production routers would be considered approved because they can only be generated by manufacturing engineers who have access to the programs required to create the production documents. Password protection ensures that only someone who is qualified and has been granted the authority to access the program can create or change the production routers. Hence, the approval is implied and can be easily verified. A similar example is drawings and design specifications that emanate from engineering CAD programs and files.

Documents Should Be Reviewed and Updated as Necessary; They Need to Be Reapproved before Being Issued

The manner in which documents are reviewed is dependent on their nature. For example, document review for procedures and work instructions can be incorporated into internal audits. When the audit occurs, the auditor verifies that the documents as written are still applicable, reflect current practices and any process changes that might have occurred, and continue to be relevant and effective. Drawings and production routers can be reviewed when a new job is issued. For service providers, instructions can be checked when a contract is renewed.

Although this is not a requirement, in some industries a log is maintained to keep track of when documents have been reviewed. The log provides the opportunity to note that a document has been reviewed on a specified date and reaffirmed to still be current, correct, and relevant.

Changes in the Document and Current Revisions Are Identified

Customers revise their specifications. Requirements change. Processes improve. It's inevitable that documents will need to be revised. Controlling and communicating document revision, therefore, is critical to your QMS. Revision status is generally indicated directly on the document. Revision levels can be denoted by alpha or numeric sequences or simply by date. Whatever method is used, ensure that it is consistently implemented. It's important that individuals know how to determine that they've got the correct revision. Requirements can change frequently in fast-paced industries. Without timely and effective communication, errors can occur. Products can be built to an obsolete specification. Orders can be shipped to the wrong address. The wrong operating instructions can be left after a field installation, or a vital piece of information can be omitted from a report. Avoiding these problems is facilitated by good revision control. As part of everyone's training, ensure that they know how to tell if they've got the right revision of a document and what they should do if they are in doubt.

The other half of this requirement deals with the revision history. ISO 9001 requires that changes be identified. For procedures and work instructions it's useful to have the revision history at the end of the document. This provides an easy reference in the event that someone wants to know what changes were made. It's also not a bad idea to archive a copy of the obsolete revision. Sometimes text is inadvertently deleted during the revision process, resulting in the loss or alteration of a requirement. Having an archived backup provides a means to go back and retrieve the lost information.

Relevant Versions of Applicable Documents Are Available Where Needed for Use

This is simply a matter of ensuring that people have access to the documents and information they need. Access does not necessarily mean that the documents must be open at their work station, although in some regulated industries this is sometimes a requirement. People need to know where to find the information.

If their documents are all electronic, they need to have appropriate access and have the ability to navigate the organization's servers to find them.

You should always try to keep the number of copies of documents to an absolute minimum. The fewer copies of documents that are floating around your organization, the smaller the chance that an obsolete document will be used.

Documents Remain Legible

This requirement seems obvious. However, it's not uncommon to see documents with approved changes that have been penciled in. It is perfectly acceptable for authorized individuals to make changes, provided they are clear and signed. Problems arise when unqualified people make changes that aren't approved or when the changes aren't legible.

There are other factors that affect the legibility of documents. Here's a list of some of the things I've observed over the years, mostly in manufacturing environments, where the same documents are reissued multiple times to the floor:

- They're soiled and grimy

- They have food or beverage stains

- The ink has smeared

- The print is faded

- There are so many notes, it's no longer possible to determine which ones are approved and/or still relevant

- They're torn at the crease lines from being folded and unfolded hundreds of times

- The edges are shredding beyond the borders and up into the area where specs are found

- They're covered with so much machine-room oil that they're becoming translucent

In many cases, the operator isn't even looking at the documents anymore, relying on his or her memory from the last time the job was run. Changes resulting from revisions or changes in personnel are missed, causing errors, delays, and unnecessary costs.

Documents of External Origin Are Identified

Documents of external origin are documents that originate from outside of your organization and contain information relating to such things as product, process, QMS, or customer requirements. You do not have the authority to approve or revise them. However, since they include requirements that you need, it's important for you to identify them and describe how they are maintained and distributed. Someone must have ownership and be able to determine if you've got the most current revision and how to get updates.

Some organizations have only one or two documents of external origin, while others have hundreds. The complexity of the process you have in place to control identification, maintenance, and distribution is directly proportional to the quantity and criticality of the documents. If your primary service is to provide equipment calibration, then the specialized instructions you might acquire from a third party for unique items will be essential to your ability to serve your customers. Similarly, in the electronics industry, the IPC standards define acceptability criteria for assemblies and printed circuit boards.

The important thing is to identify which documents of external origin your organization needs. This may be a bit challenging, since many of these documents may be scattered throughout your organization and may have been acquired without the knowledge or participation of top management or the quality department. Speak to the individuals who use them to help determine their criticality and to help you define how they are controlled. Table 5.3 shows examples of documents of external origin.

Table 5.3   Examples of documents of external origin.

International management system standards	• ISO 9001 • ISO/TS 16949 • ISO 17025 • ISO 14001
Customer specifications	• Drawings • Schematics • Bills of materials • Contractual requirement
Industry and product standards	• Clean room standard • NEMA codes • IPC standards
Statutory and regulatory requirements	• OSHA • EPA • Child Safety Protection Act • FDA
Miscellaneous	• Test standards • Calibration standards • Operating manuals • Repair manuals

Documents That Are Obsolete Must Be Identified and Prevented from Unintended Use

When a document becomes obsolete, it's important to ensure that it is discarded, properly marked as obsolete, or archived in such a manner as to ensure it is not inadvertently used. For paper copies, this is fairly simple. There are three choices: destroy them, stamp them "obsolete," or lock them away so they can't be accessed or accidentally used. For electronic documents, there are also several choices. You may overwrite the document, which achieves two purposes: It creates an approved revision and simultaneously destroys the obsolete version. Or you can print one hard copy that is retained in a secure file clearly marked as obsolete, after which you delete the electronic version. Finally, you can save obsolete versions in archive folders. This is probably the best and most efficient choice. The only concern with this practice is that security must be very robust and that access to the electronic archives must be strictly limited.

Why save obsolete versions? Why not discard them all? There are instances in which a prior revision will be needed. This is especially true in industries where revisions are common and frequent. If a product has been manufactured with embedded software, it's possible and likely that a newer version of the software will be developed for later product releases. In that case, access to previous versions would be necessary in order to troubleshoot problems or to facilitate a product transition. Sometimes in manufacturing, customers request that a product conform to a previous revision to fulfill requirements for after-market replacements parts.

Again, avoiding a proliferation of copies helps to minimize the chances of old revisions being improperly used—or of proprietary information being accidentally disclosed.

Once you've identified and sorted all your documents, it's a good idea to create a list or directory. The manner in which you structure the list can facilitate description of most recent revision, ownership, and location. Some organizations create a master document list that is developed as a simple table or spreadsheet. Others maintain an electronic directory. As with so many things in your QMS, it's important to develop a method that works for you.

The last requirement in this clause relates to the control of records. Records provide evidence that you have fulfilled the requirements found in the documents we've just discussed. Not only is that a requirement of ISO 9001, it's also helpful with a multitude of other processes. Records are indispensable to internal auditing, tracking and trending, development of goals and objectives, management review, problem investigation, and corrective action. They may also be required by your customers or by regulatory bodies.

Table 5.4 lists the records that are required by ISO 9001:2008.

Table 5.4 Records required by ISO 9001:2008.

Clause	Record required
5.6.1	Management reviews
6.2.2 (e)	Education, training, skills, and experience
7.1 (d)	Evidence that the realization processes and resulting product fulfill requirements
7.2.2	Results of the review of requirements relating to the product and actions arising from the review
7.3.2	Design and development inputs relating to product requirements
7.3.4	Results of design and development reviews and any necessary actions
7.3.5	Results of design and development verification and any necessary actions
7.3.6	Results of design and development validation and any necessary actions
7.3.7	Results of the review of design and development changes and any necessary actions
7.4.1	Results of supplier evaluations and necessary actions arising from the evaluations
7.5.2 (d)	As required by the organization to demonstrate the validation of processes for product and service provision where the resulting output cannot be verified by subsequent monitoring or measurement
7.5.3	The unique identification of the product, where traceability is a requirement
7.5.4	Customer property that is lost, damaged, or otherwise found to be unsuitable for use
7.6 (a)	Standards used for calibration or verification of measuring equipment where no international or national measurement standards exist
7.6	Validity of previous measuring results when measuring equipment is found not to conform with its requirements
7.6	Results of calibration and verification of measuring equipment

(Continued)

Table 5.4 Records required by ISO 9001:2008. (Continued)

Clause	Record required
8.2.2	Internal audit results
8.2.4	Evidence of product conformity with the acceptance criteria and indication of the authority responsible for the release of the product
8.3	Nature of the product nonconformities and any subsequent actions taken, including concessions obtained
8.5.2 (e)	Results of corrective action
8.5.3 (e)	Results of preventive action

Additionally, in 4.2.1 (d) there's a requirement to also include any other documents, including records, that are needed by the organization. For example, there are no specific requirements for maintaining records of equipment preventive maintenance. The maintenance program might be an activity that is necessary in order to ensure the continued reliability of your machinery. Records help you to calculate the return on investment for your preventive maintenance program and ensure against downtime that could impact your schedules, scrap rate, in-process defects, and on-time delivery. If your preventive maintenance process is critical to your ability to serve your customers, you should ensure proper control of those records. It's important to consider which records would be required by your organization that are not specifically mentioned in ISO 9001.

It bears noting that if you've taken an exclusion to any clause in section 7, such as design, the requirements for record retention are part of the exclusion.

ISO 9001 requires you to have a documented procedure describing how you control your records. The document needs to provide information about:

- Identification

- Storage

- Protection

- Retrieval

- Retention

- Disposition

Most organizations create a table or grid that provides easy access to the information for all the records. It's important that people who need to access the records are able to find them; otherwise, maintenance becomes a meaningless task. If records are held electronically, provide information on where and how they are stored on your servers, the path (if appropriate), and whether they require authorization for access.

Bear in mind that records that are stored electronically are vulnerable to evolutions in technology. If you have records that will need to be maintained for a prolonged period of time (20 or more years), it's worth periodically checking to make sure you have the means to access them. For example, a company might manufacture a product with a life cycle of 75 years. Over the course of a few decades, the need might arise for replacement parts. Fifteen years ago, the records may have been archived to microfiche or old-style tape drives. If the equipment to read that information has been discarded, the ability to retrieve the records has been lost.

Finally, electronic data backup is an element of document and record control and needs to be adequately defined in your documentation.

Despite the fact that there appear to be many requirements relating to document and record control, this does not have to be a complicated or onerous process. Identifying what you've got first ensures that you'll have the information to describe how your documentation works for you. It will also help you to streamline your document maintenance processes by ensuring you can find the right information when you need it.

WHAT YOU NEED TO KNOW ABOUT 4.2

You must have:

- A quality manual that includes the scope of your organization, reference to your documented procedures, and a description of the interrelation of processes

- A documented procedure describing the control of documents, taking into consideration approval, review, access, legibility, documents of external origin, protection, and obsolescence

- A documented procedure that describes how you control records, including consideration for identification, storage, protection, retrieval, retention, and disposition

6

ISO 9001:2008
Section 5

Section 5 of ISO 9001:2008 is uniquely focused on top management's responsibility. It punctuates the absolute and indisputable requirement for management's involvement. This is a responsibility that cannot be delegated or ignored.

According to the definition in Table 4.2, top management is a "person or group of people who directs and controls an organization at the highest level." In smaller organizations this function may be restricted to one individual, such as the president or owner. Top management might also consist of partners or a small management team made up of three or four individuals representing the key departments or functions. Titles might include president, vice president, CEO, CFO, COO, general manager, director, or any high-level manager. The important thing to remember is that this is considered to be the group of people who control and direct the organization. They have ownership of the requirements that are the subject of this chapter.

5.1 MANAGEMENT COMMITMENT

This requirement is actually a general statement reinforcing that it is management that owns the requirements relating to ensuring that a QMS as described in Chapter 5 is established, along with a quality policy and quality objectives. It mentions the need for management review and for allocation of resources, both of which will be discussed in greater detail later in this chapter. Finally, it touches on continual improvement, which, as has already been noted, is a QMP that should permeate the entire organization.

5.2 CUSTOMER FOCUS

Despite the fact that other individuals are often involved in communicating with customers, generating quotations, processing orders, and working on designs, it is top management that is responsible for ensuring that activities remain focused on fulfilling customer requirements.

5.3 QUALITY POLICY

Top management ensures that a quality policy is established and that it includes a statement relating to the purpose of the organization, along with a commitment to comply with the requirements of ISO 9001 and to continually improve the effectiveness of the QMS. While the latter two components are pretty generic, the first one should be unique to your organization. This part of the quality policy should state what you do. Examples might include cable and electronic harness assembly, dry cleaning, personal financial portfolio management, piano lessons, forensic lab, manufacture of nonwoven products, medical billing, or software design—just to name a few. Again, the quality policy isn't a feel-good catch phrase that could apply equally to a nuclear plant and a grocer. It has to relate to your organization.

People in the organization should understand what the policy means and be able to explain how their job helps to fulfill the intent of the quality policy. This means that top management is also responsible for ensuring that the quality policy is communicated. This can be done by posting it in prominent spots in your facility, by putting it on your Web site, and by ensuring that it's included in new hire orientations.

5.4 PLANNING

There are two things covered in this clause. The first relates to quality objectives. People tend to either misunderstand or overcomplicate this requirement. There are three things to remember. Quality objectives can relate to processes, products, or your entire system. They must be measurable. And, most important, if they're to have any meaning to you, they should relate to things you care about.

What objectives essentially say is: "This is where we are; that's where we want to be." For example, "Our current on-time delivery is 89%; we want it to be 98%." Saying you want to "get better" is not a quality objective. It's a wish. In order to have a chance at meeting your objectives, you need to know what your current status is and what you'd like the improved situation to be. Being specific and ascribing appropriate metrics helps you determine what it is you need to do, which is the subject of the second part of this clause: planning. Once you know where you want to go, you can begin planning activities, assigning tasks, and allocating resources.

The metrics don't have to be complicated. They just have to give you a reliable picture of your progress toward the goal and relate back to the purpose of the organization, as established in the quality policy. Metrics are covered in Chapter 9, which deals with monitoring and measuring. For the time being, Table 6.1 shows some examples of quality objectives. For each, it's important to identify the current status and the target—the quality objective.

Once the quality objectives have been established, they can serve as one of the many inputs into the organization's planning

Table 6.1 Examples of quality objectives.

	Now	**Objective**
At a call center:		
—Number of times phone may ring	5	2
In most manufacturing plants:		
—Scrap rate	9%	3%
—In-process reworks (per shift)	7	1
—Time to build one unit	37 minutes	29 minutes
In a forensic lab:		
—Turnaround time for drug test results	13 hours	7 hours
In a beauty salon:		
—Time before a customer is greeted	3 minutes	1 minute
For a convention planner:		
—Time to process a request for proposal	48 hours	18 hours
For a sleeping bag manufacturer:		
—Lowest temperature at which product is able to function	22°F	7°F
For a delivery service:		
—Average delivery time	145 minutes	115 minutes
For an automotive company:		
—Fuel efficiency	28 MPG	42 MPG

processes. This plan is different from the one you will put together to develop and establish your QMS—your ISO project. It's important to remember that once your QMS is established and certified, it still needs to be consistently maintained. There must be processes that allow for planning as an integral part of your commitment to continual improvement.

It's possible and likely that some planning methods are already implemented. If not, they will have to be developed.

Plans should relate to things like daily activities, improvement initiatives, customer requests, corrective actions, product improvements, and any anticipated changes.

The methods and tools you currently have in place for the ongoing planning should be consistently used and should relate to your quality policy and to improving the QMS you are establishing. Going forward, plans should reflect the review of the status of objectives and the other items required during the management review process. This will be covered later in this chapter. For the time being, it's appropriate to provide examples of some of the planning documents and records that are used to provide evidence of how the plans were developed and implemented. They include such things as:

- Strategic plans
- Project plans
- Schedules
- Gantt charts
- Building plans
- Manufacturing plans
- Designs
- Infrastructure enhancements

Appended to those plans will probably be other documents that describe the resources that you need, the expected outcome, and a completion time frame.

The only other thing to remember with this clause is the need to have plans in place so that you continue to maintain control when things are changing. For example, if you are planning to relocate your facility, it would be appropriate to have a plan for ensuring that you will be able to continue serving your customers during the move. This might include increasing stock levels, outsourcing some processes, or running parallel systems. It might involve forwarding calls to a sister division or setting up a temporary office near the new facility. There has to be evidence that you've planned the change so that your ability to fulfill customer requirements (including the defined requirements of your QMS) is not compromised.

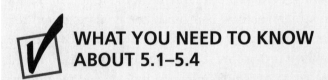

WHAT YOU NEED TO KNOW ABOUT 5.1–5.4

Top management must:

- Demonstrate a commitment to the QMS and to the fulfillment of customer requirements

- Establish the quality policy

- Ensure appropriate planning

- Ensure the establishment of measurable objectives

5.5 RESPONSIBILITY, AUTHORITY, AND COMMUNICATION

The first part of this clause if self-explanatory. You have to identify who has responsibility and authority for various aspects of your organization. Who is authorized to sign contracts? Who can override the production schedule? Who can okay a product for rework? Who can sign off on test equipment validation? Who can approve changes to documents? There are many activities for which a designated person has responsibility.

Authority and responsibility are generally identified using three different methods:

- The organizational flowchart

- Text within procedures and work instructions

- Memos, directives, and communications from top management

The second part of this clause relates to the management representative—often referred to as the ISO rep. This individual is responsible for ensuring that top management's plan for the establishment and maintenance of the QMS is implemented. He or she also reports back to management on the status of the QMS. Finally, the ISO rep ensures that individuals understand that the path to customer satisfaction lies in conforming to the requirements of ISO 9001 and conducting business within the context of a controlled QMS.

When selecting a management representative, the single most important thing to remember is that this person must be a member of the organization's management. This is not a clerical position. It cannot be delegated, nor can it be assigned to someone outside of the organization, like a consultant.

Any member of the management team can serve in this role. In a smaller organization, the president of the company may also be the management representative. Typically, the job goes to the quality manager. However, it's not uncommon to assign it to others, including the chief financial officer (CFO). This is a particularly nice fit, in that this individual tends to be the one who tracks many of the metrics that form the foundation of data used as inputs into management review. CFOs track scrap rates, rework costs, customer returns, downtime expenses, labor rates, and so forth. They also have the financial perspective that's needed when dealing with the allocation of resources, which is one of the outputs of management review. Finally, choosing someone other than the quality manager serves to discourage the attitude that this is just a "quality control thing."

The last part of this clause deals with communication. It makes sense that this requirement follows the ones relating to authority and the management representative. People must know what the expectations are and they need to know that the information comes from an authorized individual. Additionally, there must be appropriate channels for these individuals to ask questions about the organization and about things like requirements, objectives, and customer expectations. Things to consider are access to e-mails, periodic company or departmental meetings, postings, and information during orientation about any particular practices and rules for inquiries and getting information. Fulfillment of the requirements of this clause also manifests one of the quality principles: involvement of people.

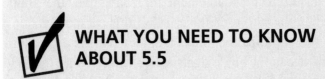

WHAT YOU NEED TO KNOW ABOUT 5.5

Top management must:

- Define responsibility and authority
- Assign a management representative
- Ensure effective internal communication

5.6 MANAGEMENT REVIEW

Top management is required to review the status and effectiveness of the organization's QMS at defined intervals. When you consider the fact that top management has ultimate responsibility for the QMS and for things like establishing objectives and ensuring fulfillment of customer requirements, periodic review makes a lot of sense. You want to know what's working and what needs more attention. And, it's important to verify that there's been ROI for the resources that were expended on action items implemented since the last review.

This is not a passive activity, with one person presenting a report that is duly filed and forgotten. It is a dynamic process where information is reviewed, objectives are revised, decisions are made, action items are assigned, resources are allocated, and plans are made for the next review.

The format and frequency of management reviews are things you decide. In larger organizations it sometimes makes sense to have teleconferences or Web-based meetings. For most small organizations the face-to-face meeting is probably the most efficient, since there are fewer participants and they're generally all located at one facility. However, that's not always the case. Some smaller organizations do have individuals operating at remote facilities. Web-based companies, design firms, and software developers, for instance, may have top managers who visit headquarters infrequently. In this case, the teleconference or Web meeting might be the most efficient option.

How often should you conduct reviews? That depends on how the reviews are structured. It's possible to have weekly meetings during which many items are discussed. However, this makes it challenging to ensure that all required items are reviewed. It also impedes your ability to analyze data relating to trends or the status of extended projects. So, the weekly meetings don't work as a management review unless they're substantiated by more complete quarterly or semiannual reviews.

There's no proscription against having only one meeting a year. However, opting for an annual meeting has more minuses than pluses. You lose the ability to respond quickly when the analysis of data reveals a downward trend. You also lose the cyclic nature of continual improvement from one review to the next. And, infrequent reviews are devalued, often treated more like a reporting function than a decision-making process. On a more positive note, it's possible to make the management review very meaningful by tying it to strategic planning and other activities like annual budget development.

The optimum for most organizations is a combination of the following:

- Informal weekly or monthly meetings where important information and decisions are recorded

- Quarterly or semiannual reviews that allow you to take a more expansive view of all the interrelated facets of your QMS, including a holistic perspective on the key decisions that were made at the less formal meetings

ISO 9001 does not specify a frequency or format. The choices are yours. You should ensure that the manner in which management review is conducted produces the greatest benefit for top management—and, ultimately, for the entire organization.

What will you review? Consider Table 6.2. On the left side are the kinds of things that top managers usually care about. On the right are the specific features of your QMS that ISO 9001 requires you to look at as part of management review. In order to make this a meaningful and effective process, the challenge

Table 6.2 Management focus vs. ISO 9001 review requirements.

Financial impact (What management cares about)	QMS effectiveness (What clause 5.6 of ISO 9001 requires for management review)
• Rework cost • Unbillable labor • Increase/decrease in sales • Waste/scrap • Cost related to customer/ regulatory complaints • Money for: — Improvement — New equipment — Marketing	• Results of audits • Customer feedback • Process performance and product conformity • Status of preventive and corrective actions • Follow-up actions from previous reviews • Changes that could affect the quality management system • Recommendations for improvement

is to present the information on the right in a manner that relates it to the concerns on the left. It's not difficult.

Here are a few examples:

- The results of audits will identify problems that are costing the organization time and money or putting it at risk with a regulatory agency.

- Process performance can be connected to quality objectives relating to cycle times, defect rates, and on-time delivery. These all impact the bottom line.

- The status of corrective actions will show whether you've addressed the problems that are costing you money and impeding your ability to serve your customers.

As with so many other aspects of your QMS, it's important not to overcomplicate things or try to invent metrics to fit the requirements. Your organization has many good practices that, properly reported, will fulfill most of the requirements of this clause of the standard. Some metrics that are gathered will cover more than one category. For example, corrective actions resulting from customer returns will be at least part of the input to three categories: customer feedback, product conformity, and corrective actions.

Table 6.3 shows tips and examples for each category. They should not be considered mandatory or all-inclusive. The only requirement is that the review must include all of the category headings, which are derived from subclause 5.6.2 of ISO 9001:2008.

In order for a management review to be complete, several things must occur:

- Analysis of information relating to each of the required categories

- Decision on what action(s) to take

- Allocation of resources and authorization to proceed

- Establishment or creation of quality objectives, as appropriate

- Records of all of the above

Table 6.3   Tips and examples for management review.

Results of audits[1]		
Types of audits	**What to review**	**Possible decisions**
• Internal audits • Customer audits • Regulatory inspections • Third-party (registrar and certification body) assessments	• Problems • Risks and potential problems • Opportunities for improvement • Benchmarks	• Issue request for corrective action • Initiate preventive action • Implement improvement projects
Customer feedback[2]		
Types of feedback	**What to review**	**Possible decisions**
• Returns • Complaints (including those that don't result in returned product) • Testimonials/ compliments • Repeat sales • Opportunities to quote on new projects • Market research • Industry recognition • Surveys	• Problems • Trends • Risks • Opportunities for improvement	• Issue request for corrective action • Explore new markets • Acquire new technology • Adjust schedules and capacity for changing demand • Implement improvement projects

(Continued)

Table 6.3　Tips and examples for management review. (Continued)

Process performance and product conformity[3]		
Processes or products	**What to review**	**Possible decisions**
• In-process defects • Rework costs • Scrap rate • On-time delivery • Cycle time • Inventory levels/ turns • Downtime • Process yields	• Trends • Problems • Cost overruns • Waste • Bottlenecks • Quality objectives	• Issue request for corrective action • Acquire new technology • Conduct training • Adjust schedules and capacity for changing demand • Adjust quality objectives • Implement improvement projects
Status of preventive and corrective actions[4]		
Corrective and preventive actions	**What to review**	**Possible decisions**
• Corrective actions • Preventive actions	• Effectiveness • Closure • Trends • Points of origin • Problems solved • Risks mitigated • Solution benchmarks • Money saved	• Bench new practices • Communicate lessons learned • Conduct training • Identify opportunities • Implement improvement projects
Follow-up actions from previous management reviews[5]		
Actions from previous reviews	**What to review**	**Possible decisions**
• Any actions from previous management reviews	• Status • Results • Effectiveness • ROI	• Ongoing work • Track and trend • Closeout • Identify further opportunities • Adjust quality objectives

(Continued)

Table 6.3 Tips and examples for management review. (Continued)

Changes that could affect the quality management system		
Kinds of changes	**What to review**	**Possible decisions**
• Relocation • Changes to regulatory requirements • New product line • New technology • Changes to environmental rules or local ordinances • Loss of a major supplier	• Status • Risk • Impact on organization	• Monitor situation • Outsource processes • Acquire new technology • Increase capacity • Develop plan to address new EPA rules • Conduct training • Research alternate suppliers
Recommendations for improvement		
Origins of recommendations	**What to review**	**Possible decisions**
• Employee suggestion box • Outputs from analysis of data • Ideas from self-directed teams • Consultants • Industry experts	• Value (anticipated ROI) • Benefit (process or product improvement?) • Feasibility • Cost • Constraints	• Monitor situation • Request more detailed plan • Authorize action and allocate necessary resources • Determine recommendation is not actionable

[1] Note that ISO 9001 does not restrict this category to internal audits.

[2] A combination of several items on this list should yield a clear representation of the status of customer satisfaction, as well as areas that need improvement.

[3] You should find most of the quality objectives that you have established and are monitoring tied to this category.

[4] There is no need to look at every individual action, unless there are very few. It's more beneficial to highlight the significant ones and summarize the status and the results of the others.

[5] You should have clear traceability of action items from the review in which they originate to the review at which they are determined to be closed out.

WHAT YOU NEED TO KNOW ABOUT 5.6

Top management must:

- Conduct reviews of the system to ensure its effectiveness

- Plan for improvements

- Allocate the necessary resources

7

ISO 9001:2008
Section 6

S ection 6 of ISO 9001:2008 deals with the resources that are necessary to implement and maintain the QMS. As we saw in the last chapter, management has responsibility for the allocation of resources. This is done through planning processes and as an output of management review.

Any organization, regardless of its nature, needs resources to function. The first part of this section makes general statements about the fact that the organization must identify and provide the necessary resources to meet customer requirements and to ensure fulfillment of the requirements of the QMS. These relate to things such as tools, documents, raw materials, people, and, as appropriate, work environment. Most of the requirements end up being further described in the documents that deal directly with each process. Manufacturing instructions will mention tooling, equipment, safety requirements, materials, and so forth. Engineering processes will refer to the CAD files, prototype lab, and project documents.

There are three groups of resource requirements that are elaborated in this section: people, infrastructure, and work environment.

6.2 COMPETENCE, TRAINING, AND AWARENESS

There are several requirements in this clause. Many people focus exclusively on the training part of this clause, which can actually end up creating more work and eventually less value. It can also result in a failure to fulfill some important but fairly easy requirements.

The first part of this clause deals with awareness. This was touched on briefly in the preceding chapter. The organization has to ensure that individuals are aware of the role they play in fulfilling customer requirements. This is accomplished through effective communication of the quality policy, quality objectives, and information about people's tasks and responsibilities.

The next thing to consider is the element of competence. By properly addressing the requirements related to competence, an organization can decrease the amount of time spent generating documents related to training. This can also decrease the number of how-to documents that clog your system.

Assessing competence involves determining what a person needs to be able to do in order to perform a task properly, such as process an order. Part of this work is already built into many job descriptions. For example, as part of the hiring process, individuals' telephone etiquette, computer skills, and organizational skills may be assessed to verify that they are able to handle the job. This establishes that they have the necessary competence.

Once a person is hired, orientation and on-the-job training are conducted. At the end of a specified period of time, the individual must demonstrate the ability to perform the tasks without error. When order processors have demonstrated the ability to perform the following tasks successfully, they are deemed both competent and qualified:

- Take a phone order from a customer, collecting the following information:

  — Product

  — Quantity

  — Shipping information

  — Delivery date

  — Special instructions

- Ensure the ability to fulfill customer requirements

  — Check stock and manufacturing schedule

  — Verify the ability to meet customer delivery date

- Input the order into a computer

- Generate and e-mail an acknowledgment to the customer

The requisite competence is built into the job description. And a checklist of items used to demonstrate qualification, along with the prompts built into the order processing software, replace work instructions for many mundane tasks, removing the need for documents that will rarely be read after the on-the-job training is complete.

In some instances, individuals will arrive with credentials that attest to their competence. They may have industry certifications, university degrees, or a resume attesting to years of experience. They do not need to be "trained" to be chemists or programmers or engineers or accountants.

The organization has to determine what training is needed. Training requirements originate from several predictable needs:

- Someone arrives with the requisite competence but needs training on specific tasks

- A decision is made to cross-train individuals to augment organizational capability

- New equipment, software, or processes are introduced that require training

- A process, like a safety protocol, requires periodic refresher training

Determining what training is needed is a great output of management review. For example, say you decide to add a second shift and promote a group leader from the day shift to the position of evening supervisor. That individual will need training on scheduling, managing workflow, handling problems, and reporting daily tallies. This training is a resource.

ISO 9001 also requires that you be able to evaluate the effects of the training. In the example above, the filled-out checklist would constitute evidence that the on-the-job training was effective in getting the desired results: the demonstrated ability of the order processor to perform the task. This method works in most instances. However, for some activities, there may be a need for a test or some other verifiable method. In the electronic assembly industry, it's typical for individuals to complete a test at the end of their IPC training. Some self-directed online courses have tests built into them. Some jobs, like truck driver or electrician, also require a valid license.

While you don't want to overcomplicate this process, it's important to have some form of verification activity for training. Saying "we haven't had a problem yet" does not demonstrate effectiveness. It may just mean you've been lucky. One error could result in a major product defect. Having a method of verifying that people know how to do things could save you lots of money.

This takes us to the last requirement of this clause. There must be records that provide evidence that you've verified competence, determined training needs (this can be part of management review), conducted training, and evaluated effectiveness.

WHAT YOU NEED TO KNOW ABOUT 6.2

You must:

- Ensure people's awareness of their role in meeting customer requirements

- Determine necessary competence

- Decide what training needs to be offered

- Provide the training

- Evaluate the results of the training

- Keep records

6.3 INFRASTRUCTURE AND 6.4 WORK ENVIRONMENT

The requirements of 6.3 and 6.4 are often merged in small organizations. What is required is that you ensure the adequate provision and maintenance of the facility, work space, equipment, and support services like vehicles and communication systems.

The extent of the control and the need to have processes in place are reliant on the criticality of each factor. For example, say a manufacturing plant has hundreds of pieces of production equipment. There are several of each kind, meaning they've got redundancy built into their workload capacity. Another manufacturer has one or two very specialized and highly automated machines. The manner in which each organization develops its equipment maintenance program may be markedly different. In the first example, work can be shifted to other machines, minimizing downtime. So, lapses in preventive maintenance might not carry any great risk. The second manufacturer could be out of business for several days if a machine goes down, resulting in dozens of lost labor hours and the eventuality of late deliveries. The need to ensure optimum reliable performance and mitigate the likelihood of machine failure will mandate a more robust preventive maintenance program.

Similarly, one organization may have a small van used for local pickups and deliveries, whereas another has a highly specialized truck equipped with tools, diagnostic instrumentation, and materials needed to do field repairs. The vehicle maintenance program should reflect the criticality of the processes related to the vehicles. Other examples, as appropriate to various industries, might include adequate telecommunications capacity to handle customer technical support or servers capable of handling e-commerce.

The work environment requirements are a direct link to the infrastructure requirements. If product must be manufactured in a temperature- and humidity-controlled environment, then the HVAC equipment for the facility must meet specific requirements.

Following are examples of the kinds of things you may need to consider as appropriate to your industry. Again, the level and extent of control are reliant on how critical these features are to your ability to meet customer requirements:

- Temperature

- Humidity

- Air filtration/Control of airborne contaminants

- Clean room environments

- Lighting

- Hygiene/Cleanliness

- Pest control

- Hazmat considerations

- Electrostatic discharge (ESD) protocols

- Weather protection for processes conducted outdoors

- Adequate space

- Noise mitigation

- Distraction-free environment

- Ergonomics

WHAT YOU NEED TO KNOW ABOUT 6.3 AND 6.4

You must, as appropriate to your industry:

- Ensure that the infrastructure, including equipment, telecommunications, and transport, is adequate and properly controlled

- Ensure that the environments in which processes are conducted and products are produced are applicable and adequate to ensure the integrity of the product and processes

8

ISO 9001:2008
Section 7

Section 7 of ISO 9001:2008 deals with all of the activities that are directly related to producing products (including services) and delivering them to the customer. It is the part of the business that most people think of when asked about their processes. And it relates to the elements of your QMS that are most uniquely yours. These are the processes that often distinguish you from your competition.

It's in this section of ISO 9001 that we see how this standard can be so generic as to have global applicability while at the same time so precise as to allow for uniform implementation and conformity. Regardless of your location or industry, you are still required to have processes (as appropriate to your industry) that address such things as understanding customer requirements, design, qualifying suppliers, controlling production processes, identification and traceability, storage, packaging, and delivery.

This is the only section of the standard for which you can claim an exclusion. If, for example, you do not conduct design, calibrate equipment, or handle customer-owned materials, you are not required to have processes or documentation for those activities. This is discussed in Chapter 4.

7.1 PLANNING FOR PRODUCT REALIZATION

This clause basically reiterates what was discussed in Chapter 6. ISO 9001 requires planning for processes and activities. In this clause, the plans relate specifically to making (or "realizing") product. It's probable that most organizations already have much of this planning in place. For example, you may have plans that include:

- Running an MRP (material requirements planning) report and using it to plan what will be purchased for upcoming jobs

- Design or design change plans

- Development of project plans with customers

- Schedules

- Creation of production routers (also called travelers or run tickets)

- Assembly of document packages that define all the steps to fulfill a service contract

These are your product realization plans. Within them should be found, as appropriate, objectives, documents and resources required, monitoring, inspection or test methods, and evidence of fulfillment of tasks and the resulting acceptable product.

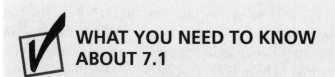

WHAT YOU NEED TO KNOW ABOUT 7.1

You must, as appropriate to your industry:

- Have plans that define various steps in the process of producing your product

7.2 CUSTOMER-RELATED PROCESSES

The first part of this clause deals with understanding customer requirements. In small organizations this is usually not a complex process. With catalog items it's simply a matter of confirming the part number and description with the customer, verifying quantity, checking stock, and determining delivery. For a service, such as auto glass replacement, the process might be to ask the customer about the make and model of their vehicle, which window needs to be replaced, whether the repair will be done at their home or whether the car will be brought into the facility, what time is mutually convenient, and whether the replacement is covered by their insurance policy.

Some small organizations do become involved in more elaborate customer requirements. In some cases, detailed specifications must be reviewed, materials researched, quotations received from multiple suppliers, estimated build documents developed, acceptance criteria established, and special requirements for labeling and packaging defined.

Additionally, you have to ensure the inclusion of features that are required by statutory and regulatory requirements but may not be mentioned by the customer. For example, if you are giving a customer a quote on wiring an addition to their home, you need to ensure that all local codes are incorporated into the job, regardless of whether the customer has specified them in the request.

The concept of "product" includes all the deliverables the customer requests. Organizations often exclude from the product such things as packaging or delivery date. When specified by the customer, however, these constitute part of the customer's requirements. Following are things that may need to be considered when seeking to understand customer requirements:

- Features of the product
- Options

- Quantity

- Required delivery

- Certifications or other documents that need to accompany the product

- Traceability of materials or components

- Labeling

- Packaging

- Independent third-party reports

- Processes carried out under contractually agreed-upon conditions

- Use of mandated suppliers and outsourced process providers

The second part of this clause deals with the acceptance of a tender, contract, or order. Once an order is accepted, it's important to verify that there are no discrepancies between what was quoted and what is being ordered. For some organizations, quoting and order processing are a combined activity. In other organizations, there may be a lag time of several weeks between the formal quote and the receipt of a customer order. In those instances, it might be necessary to reverify the availability of components, recheck the production schedule, and ensure that the customer has not revised any specifications. If there are discrepancies, there must be evidence that they've been resolved. E-mail has become one of the most common methods of retaining these kinds of records.

Finally, there should be a contingency in your documents that describes the process in the event that a customer changes an order once it's been released for production.

The last part of this clause addresses the establishment of effective methods of communication with your customer. Things to consider include:

- The location of e-mails from customers that contain contract or specification information

- Who in your facility is authorized to speak with customers concerning the acceptance of orders, changes to orders, and concessions

- How customer complaints are handled

 WHAT YOU NEED TO KNOW ABOUT 7.2

You must:

- Understand customer requirements

- Take into account statutory and regulatory requirements not mentioned by the customer

- Verify ability to fulfill customer requirements

- Ensure that discrepancies are resolved before an order is processed

- Have a contingency for changes, amendments, and cancellations

- Provide an effective method of communicating with the customer

7.3 DESIGN AND DEVELOPMENT

With a few notable exceptions, most small organizations either don't get involved in design or have very basic design processes. However, with the proliferation of ISO 9001 into many nonmanufacturing settings, there are more small organizations doing design. They include small research and development firms, interior decorators, schools (curriculum development), event planners, and test labs (designing and developing test methods as a product).

This is a lengthy clause with many requirements. Some of the subclauses can be combined. For example, the two involving verification and validation can occur simultaneously, although that is not always the case. Similarly, the final review may also encompass verification and validation.

The following sections provide more specific information on each subclause.

Design and Development Planning

It's important to know how your design and development process will be implemented. Things to include in your plan are how the process is initiated, who is involved, the identification of stages in the process, the contingency for changes to the design, and the appropriate involvement of other individuals at appropriate points in the design process.

This last category—involving individuals—bears further elaboration. It's vital to ensure that people who may have responsibility for later parts of the design or the ultimate product are not excluded. For example, an engineer may have selected a component from a new supplier who has not been qualified by the purchasing department. Although the prototype furnished is fabulous, it isn't until the organization goes into full production that it learns that the supplier does not have the capacity to produce the large quantity of parts that will be needed. Involving the purchasing department at an earlier stage would have ensured that the supplier was vetted and the capacity issue addressed sooner through an on-site visit or a comparable qualification process. Similarly, the design engineers may have developed a new method of assembling a product. Unfortunately, they didn't involve the operations manager, who needed to purchase and install new equipment, rewrite assembly instructions, and train 40 people on the new process. All relevant features that affect product conformance to requirements and its function must be included in the design. So it may be appropriate to include warehouse managers for environmentally sensitive materials or shipping personnel for perishable products.

Design and Development Inputs

What are the requirements that must be fulfilled for this design? Where do they come from? It's appropriate to use the following as design inputs:

- Specifications from the customer
- Information from previous products and design projects
- Market inputs
- Statutory and regulatory requirements

These requirements should be adequately defined and clear enough to enable the design process and to allow for specific verification that the outputs match what was desired. They should encompass all appropriate aspects of the product, including consideration for such factors as labeling, life cycle, and packaging.

Design and Development Outputs

This subclause requires you to define what you expect the output of the design process to be, including the methods used to verify against the design input. It also requires you to ensure that the design outputs are communicated to individuals who have responsibility for post-design activities.

Design and Development Review

The design must be reviewed at defined stages. These reviews usually coincide with identified milestones in the project. For simple products there may be only one review. Essentially, reviews help to ensure that you're staying on track.

The reviews should involve all interested parties. They should assess whether desired milestones and outputs have been achieved or should result in other decisions as to how to proceed. This could include reverting to a less ambitious product objective, redefining a requirement, or removing a particular feature. Changes to the design plan may involve revisiting results from previous reviews, revising the design plan (and schedule), or contacting individuals who signed off on earlier reviews.

Design and Development Verification

The design verification requires you to ensure that the final design matches what was in the original design plan and that it conforms to the design output, meaning that it has met the acceptance criteria of the design project.

Design and Development Validation

Validation differs from verification in that it ensures that the product functions as intended. It's one thing to have a device perform in a test lab; it's another matter to ensure it works in a different environment, under different conditions, or when integrated with other equipment or legacy software. For example, it's possible for an electrical device to function in North America but not in Europe due to variances in electric currents.

As previously mentioned, sometimes verification and validation occur concurrently.

Design and Development Changes

Think of design change as an abbreviated design process. In this case, you perform only those tasks that relate to the change. You can incorporate any steps from the original design that are still valid.

Interfaces with other interested parties still need to be considered. If the change is dimensional or cosmetic, you might not have to involve purchasing or inventory management. Conversely, if the design change involves components, then purchasing and inventory management are two groups you will definitely want to involve.

Finally, for all phases of the design process, ensure that you maintain records of actions taken and results.

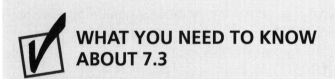

WHAT YOU NEED TO KNOW ABOUT 7.3

You must:

- Develop your design plan

- Define the inputs and outputs of the design

- Ensure the appropriate involvement of key personnel

- Conduct design reviews

- Have a contingency for changes resulting from design reviews

- Perform verification and validation of the design

7.4 PURCHASING

There are three unique requirements in this clause. You must qualify the suppliers from which you procure materials, components, and services. You must have a controlled purchasing process. And you must have acceptance criteria for what is purchased.

Defined and controlled selection and qualification of suppliers is how you ensure the integrity of your supply chain, which in turn helps ensure your ability to meet your customers' requirements. If you can't get parts, materials, or services, you can't get product out to market. Or, if parts are defective or late, your organization incurs the costs associated with reworks, replacing parts, and the inevitable effect on delivery to the customer.

Some suppliers are more critical than others. Some have more risk associated with them than others. The qualification process should be proportionate to criticality and risk. You may wish to have more than one method of qualifying your suppliers. For example, you may have three categories: generic, low-value, off-the-shelf components; made-to-order parts; and outsourced or secondary processes. For the first category, qualification could be as simple as requiring evidence of an ISO certificate or completion of a questionnaire attesting to capacity, key processes, and ability to meet your product requirements. For the made-to-order items, the qualification might be more robust depending on how specialized and complex the parts are. In some cases, an ISO certificate plus a sample run might be required. Or, it might be determined that the criticality of the components warrants an on-site audit. The same rationale is used for the third category. Some outsourced processes like repackaging carry low risk, while others, like etching or machining, might be of greater concern. The qualification of suppliers of outsourced processes may be part of the control of outsourced processes discussed in Chapter 5.

ISO 9001 does not require you to have an approved supplier list. However, this is the usual method for denoting those suppliers who have been qualified. It's simple and easily accessible. The standard requires you to keep records of the results of your qualification activities. The ubiquitous list fills the bill nicely. But it's not the only way of recording that a supplier is qualified. Increasingly, organizations are using a designated field in their supplier database to tick off the status of suppliers. Rather than accessing a list that needs to be monitored and updated, they just check to see that the "approved" box in the database is checked off.

Finally, there has to be a method of determining whether suppliers continue to perform and provide materials to specified requirements. Things that should be monitored, depending on the criticality of the supplied product and the applicability to your business, include:

- Quality of product

- On-time delivery

- Response to inquiries or technical support

- Provision of required certificates or test reports

- Conformance to any other specified requirements (labeling, package size, use of special equipment, adherence to defined procedures, lot traceability, etc.)

The next thing that is covered in this clause is the actual procurement of the product. Your purchase orders must include adequate information about what is being ordered. If the product is being manufactured to a drawing, it's appropriate to ensure that both the drawing number and the revision level are included in the purchasing documents. The drawing may have been previously submitted as part of the quoting process, or a copy should accompany the order. If there are additional requirements for certificates of conformance, independent test results, special packaging, or labeling, these must also be included on the purchase order. For services, all the deliverables might be specified in a contract. Or, if you send staff out for industry-required training, the instruction provider's registration form will specify how many people are being trained; the time, date, and location of the training; the nature of the course; and the certification or proof-of-training documents that will be issued.

All of this ensures that both parties have agreed on the requirements and the product to be furnished. The better the job you do of communicating your needs to your suppliers, the fewer errors and problems you'll encounter. Effective implementation of your purchasing processes is a manifestation of the eighth quality management principle: mutually beneficial supplier relations.

The last part of this clause deals with acceptance criteria for purchased products. It is not necessary to inspect and test everything. However, it is necessary to define how you determine whether you've received what you've ordered. For off-the-shelf items this may be as simple as checking the information on the outside of the carton. For secondary processes, like heat treating, it could be by receipt of a certificate verifying that the product meets certain ASTM requirements. Raw material is often verified by reviewing a certificate of analysis. Calibration is similarly accepted by review of the certification that accompanies the instruments coming back from the calibration provider.

For other items, it may be necessary to establish inspection or test processes. You get to decide what dimensions are considered critical or what other features like color and weight need to be checked. You may select a sampling plan that defines how many out of each lot will be inspected. This sampling must make sense and reflect the intent, which is to ensure that the product is okay. You can develop your own sampling plan or utilize one that is publicly available. The most common sampling plan used is ANSI/ASQ Z1.4 (the old Mil Spec 105E).

The bottom line is you must have a method of determining that you got what you ordered. It's just common sense.

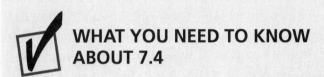

WHAT YOU NEED TO KNOW ABOUT 7.4

You must:

- Qualify your suppliers

- Have a list or other method for denoting which suppliers are qualified

- Ensure that the information on purchasing documents is clear, correct, and complete

- Have established methods for inspecting product or otherwise determining that it is acceptable

7.5 PRODUCTION AND SERVICE PROVISION

There are multiple subclauses in this part of ISO 9001. They relate to the actual making of the product or provision of the service.

Control of Production and Service Provision

Control requires that you adequately define the activities and characteristics of the product and that you ensure that you have appropriate equipment and tools, qualified people, a suitable environment, and methods for determining whether the product conforms. Section 6 covers the requirements for properly managing resources. In section 7, the requirements relate to how those resources are used.

As was mentioned earlier, in a manufacturing environment, information about manufacturing product is often encompassed in a production traveler or packet of production documents. It may include such things as a bill of materials for kitting assembly parts, a drawing, a machine profile, an inspection form, labeling directions, and other help guides. In addition, there may be work instructions or industry specifications. For a field installation, the information in the packet will have instructions, the contract, a list of replacement parts, a check sheet, and a customer sign-off form. For a hotel housekeeper, it will include the schedule of rooms to clean, the refreshment bar inventory sheet, a checklist of tasks completed, a form to request engineering if there's a problem, and perhaps (for trainees) diagrams showing how the coffee station and bathroom amenities are supposed to be laid out. In terms of resources, the activities will be assigned to qualified individuals who will be provided with the necessary tools and equipment. In the case of the manufacturing example, there will be production equipment and tools for measurement; for the field installation, there will be a field kit; and for the hotel housekeeper there will be cleaning supplies and a cart with replacement stock.

The last thing mentioned under this heading is the need to establish and implement appropriate control of post-delivery processes.

Validation of Processes for Production and Service Provision

The validation part of the standard deals with the kinds of processes where the product cannot be verified after it is manufactured or delivered. This includes cases where testing would result in the destruction of the product. These processes are often referred to as "special processes."

Examples of special processes include:

- Welding

- Soldering

- Painting

- Concrete casting

- Forging

- Epoxying

- Coiling or winding of materials

In all cases, the product cannot be tested without damaging or destroying it. Therefore, since you can't verify the product, you must validate the process. By ensuring appropriate control of the process, in effect you guarantee the integrity of the resulting product. There are several methods of achieving adequate control. It may be necessary to employ more than one to ensure product integrity. Examples of methods of controlling these processes include:

- The process may only be performed by individuals who have been certified or specially trained—and whose skills are periodically reverified.

- The measuring equipment that controls the process must be calibrated or reverified at defined intervals. Examples include pressure gages, thermostats, voltage meters, and footage counters (for winders).

- The process can only be carried out in controlled environments like clean rooms, electrostatic discharge (ESD) protected areas, or temperature-controlled spaces.

- The material used for the process must be certified.

- The process must be carried out using industry-specific requirements.

For service industries, we can look to the hotel example again. Assume that one of the services (products) is to provide wake-up calls for guests. It's not possible to test ahead of time whether the automated system for the 4:30 a.m. wake-up call is working properly without actually waking the guest up. However, it is possible to run simulations and validate that the software that controls the automated system is working properly.

In all cases, the important thing to remember is that if you can't verify the product, you must be able to validate the process.

Identification and Traceability

It's important that product be identified and that its inspection status be known at all stages of product realization. For some organizations, this is fairly straightforward. The material is tagged or is identified by production documentation that follows it through the entire process. In other instances, a combination of methods can be used. The parts have an identification, but the inspection status is denoted by its location. Material that has passed inspection is placed on a designated bench awaiting the next operation. Its location indicates its status. Other organizations use different colored dots, stickers, temporary marks, or acceptance tags.

Traceability requirements vary greatly and are often not applicable. However, where it is required, it's necessary to maintain appropriate records. Examples of traceability include lot traceability (for manufacturing), material certifications or country of origin data, patient information (for medical labs), chain of custody for evidence (for forensic labs), and student transcripts (for educational institutions).

Serialization of finished products or components is another aspect of traceability. This is generally specified by the customer or incorporated into the design and development process. Due to its specificity, the manner in which the serialization is recorded and the method of retrieval will be unique to the product or customer. Serial numbers for components may be recorded on production documentation. For finished goods, the numbers may be in either a manual log or a database.

Customer Property

When customers provide some of their own property in the form of either components or tooling, the organization has to ensure that the material is identified and protected. The standard further requires appropriate communication with customers in the event their property is lost or destroyed or becomes unusable.

This is another one of the subclauses that is often claimed as an exclusion. However, if you do have customer property, the level of control is dependent on the amount you have and its value. In a repair shop or a dry cleaner, the customer furnishes you with their property. Your business is 100% dependent on the customer providing you with their property. Your product is the repaired device or cleaned garment. Therefore, in these cases, this requirement is particularly important and your processes should be proportionately robust. Similarly, a financial portfolio management firm must have extensive processes in place to safeguard the personal information its clients entrust to it. ISO 9001 has a note in this section stating: "Customer property can include intellectual property or personal data."

Another company might have only one customer who furnishes a special decal with their logo or custom packaging. In this case, the process is infrequent, and, although important, it does not require the same level of identification, monitoring, and control.

The requirement also includes items that may be needed to manufacture, test, preserve, or ship the product. Customer property that would require control includes such things as:

- Raw material
- Components
- Tooling
- Jigs

- Test fixtures
- Packaging
- Labels
- Proprietary information
- Personal data

Methods of control could include:

- Proper identification
- Periodic cycle counting
- Limited access
- Locked storage
- Appropriate storage (for environmentally sensitive material)
- Electronic security (for data)

Finally, some industries have post-delivery or after-market processes. For example, as part of the contract for the sale of an office copier, an organization might agree to free maintenance for one year. Or, a software company might agree to furnish product updates on a monthly basis for a specified period of time. This requirement only relates to activities that are contractually agreed features of the product. It does not deal with returns or warranty repairs, which are covered in section 8 of ISO 9001.

Preservation of Product

This part of 7.5 relates to the handling, storage, shipping, and protection of product. It's important that material be stored in a suitable environment. Whereas section 6 discusses a suitable environment as a resource to be managed, this subclause speaks to how that environment is utilized to ensure conforming product during internal processes and when the product is stored.

Material and finished goods should be identified and stored in a manner that ensures they are protected from adverse conditions that could cause them to degrade. For most organizations, an area that is clean and protected from the weather is adequate. However, some products must be stored under very specific environmental conditions. This could relate to temperature, humidity, air filtration, or security.

Handling is usually just a matter of implementing good practices. However, there are specific requirements for handling certain materials. Electronic components often require ESD protocols; delicate parts may need to be handled with gloves.

How product is packaged and delivered also varies by industry. For most manufactured items, ensuring that parts are adequately packed to protect them from damage while in transit is all that is required. Other products must be wrapped in ESD packaging, shipped in refrigerated trucks, packed in specially designed tubes, stacked on prequalified pallets, or shipped in hazmat containers. If the product is a test lab report, an updated financial portfolio, or software, the most important aspect of the delivery may be its security.

WHAT YOU NEED TO KNOW ABOUT 7.5

You must:

- Plan and implement the activities to produce product, including providing necessary resources, defining the sequence of steps, and monitoring the process and its output

- Validate any process where the outcome cannot be verified after it's completed

- Identify product

- When required, have defined methods of providing traceability

- Identify and protect customer property

- Ensure product is properly handled, stored, and packaged

- When applicable, control post-delivery processes

7.6 CONTROL OF MONITORING AND MEASUREMENT EQUIPMENT

This part of the standard is usually referred to as the calibration clause. It's actually more—and perhaps less—than calibration, depending on the quantity, complexity, and variety of the equipment, its criticality, and your industry. ISO 9001 requires an organization to have adequate control of the equipment used to verify product conformity. This also includes equipment used to control processes that may affect product conformity (this was discussed earlier, in the section on validation of processes). The equipment must be identified and its calibration status known.

In manufacturing environments, the most common method of controlling measuring equipment is through calibration. If calibration is being done, it's important to define the calibration process. For instruments calibrated in-house, the process should describe the method used, the standard utilized (for example, set of gage blocks), the acceptable range, and the frequency of calibration. If the calibrations are carried out by a third party, the selection and qualification of the calibration provider could fall into one of the categories mentioned in the purchasing clause. Ensuring that calibrations are carried out by a qualified third party becomes a large portion of your control of this process. Calibrations must be traceable to national or international standards such as NIST (National Institute of Standards and Technology).

Some equipment may just need to be verified prior to use. In this case, the equipment (often a vernier or caliper) is checked against a gage block or pin gage whose calibration status is known.

If a product undergoes multiple operations, it might be acceptable to use "reference only" equipment for the rough dimensions, since the final product will be verified using calibrated equipment. Some things get periodically checked and, if they become worn or defective, are simply discarded. This might include disposable color samples, pipettes, and tape measures.

Apart from the traditionally calibrated equipment like micrometers, calipers, thread gages, comparators, and digital indicators, there is a whole array of other items that need to be controlled. Here is a brief list:

- Gages

- Known good samples

- Jigs

- pH meters

- Test software

- Oscilloscopes

- Torque wrenches

- Color charts

- Crimpers

In each instance it's important to determine what is being measured and decide the most effective way of controlling the equipment in order to ensure product conformity.

Another thing that's covered in this clause is ensuring that the equipment is capable of measuring the requisite feature or dimension. If a drawing calls out a tolerance of ± .005, then a caliper that can only read to two decimal places will not be capable of verifying the dimension. Checking this during the quoting process will ensure that, if there's a need to procure a new gage, it's identified and built into the cost. Also, equipment must be suitably protected from degradation, invalidation, or unintended adjustment. Basically, you must ensure that equipment is properly handled and stored.

Finally, records must be kept. The main purpose of the records is to be able to check the validity of previous calibrations in the event a piece of equipment is found to be out of calibration. This would address any concern that product may have been deemed acceptable and shipped to the customer based on a measurement using the suspect device. In turn, this would help the organization decide what action to take, if any.

Control of monitoring and measuring equipment also includes consideration for test software. Depending on the nature of the software, it may be necessary to validate it or to utilize periodic self-diagnostics. Some of the security features built into your electronic documentation control programs and back-up protocols may be used to ensure control of monitoring and measurement software.

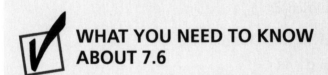

WHAT YOU NEED TO KNOW ABOUT 7.6

You must:

- Identify equipment used to accept product or control processes that affect product conformity

- Maintain and calibrate, reverify, revalidate, or periodically check equipment

- Define methods used

- Keep records of calibration or the results of other actions taken to control the equipment

- Ensure equipment is capable of making the necessary measurements

- Protect equipment from damage or unintended adjustment

- Check previous records in the event a piece of equipment is found to be out of calibration or out of conformance

9

ISO 9001:2008
Section 8

Section 8 of ISO 9001:2008 covers the various processes and activities that organizations use to check how they're doing and the subsequent improvement actions taken based on what they discover. Activities related to the "check" and "act" segments of the PDCA cycle (discussed in Chapter 3) reside in this part of the standard.

The first part has general language about the need to measure product conformity and the effectiveness of the QMS and to use that information to initiate action to improve them both.

8.2 MONITORING AND MEASUREMENT

Clause 8.2 is divided into four parts: the measurement of customer satisfaction, the assessment of the organization through internal audits, the monitoring and measurement of processes, and the monitoring and measurement of product.

Customer Satisfaction

ISO 9001:2008 is primarily focused on fulfilling customer requirements. The degree to which an organization achieves this endeavor is the measure of customer satisfaction. Therefore, it's essential to have processes in place to measure customer satisfaction and customers' perceptions of how well the organization is meeting their requirements.

There are many ways of assessing customer satisfaction. Some organizations have been led to believe that they are required to conduct surveys. While this is a good method in some industries, the practice does not lend itself universally to all. In some markets, customer inclination to respond to surveys is erratic, resulting in unreliable and incomplete information. Any information gathered is proportionately skewed to reflect the feedback from the small subset that has chosen to respond, rather than customers overall. Also, small organizations tend to have fewer customers and often have more intimate relationships with them. Because it's often the case that the owners and managers are also the primary interface with customers, interviews and personal contacts are probably a more reliable barometer of how customers view your organization's performance.

It's important to remember that the absence of complaints is not synonymous with customer satisfaction. Some customers simply choose another vendor rather than continuing to do business with an organization that has failed to adequately fulfill their needs.

Customer satisfaction can be assessed by looking at multiple factors. The basic data that you'll need are probably already available from other information that is being tracked. You may assess your customers' level of satisfaction by using a combination of any of the following:

- Interviews
- Surveys
- Complaints and returns
- Compliments and testimonials
- Industry publications/consumer reports
- Warranty claims

- Repeat business/loss of business
- Opportunity to quote on new projects
- Focus groups

A balanced look at several of these inputs should yield a reasonable profile of how you're doing. This should provide reliable information that can be used to plan and take action.

Internal Audits

If you can get beyond the negative baggage that surrounds the internal auditing process, it should yield great information on the status of processes and your QMS overall.

ISO 9000:2005 defines an audit as a "systematic, independent and documented process for obtaining audit evidence and evaluating it objectively to determine the extent to which audit criteria are fulfilled." The audit criteria are contained in the requirements of ISO 9001:2008 (and by extension those found in your own procedures and documents) and in the requirements of your customer. Since the system you've implemented is based on what you identified and established as necessary to meet your customer's requirements, it stands to reason that the more closely you comply with the requirements of your QMS, the better shot you have of meeting your goals.

As mentioned in Chapter 5, internal auditing is one of the six documented procedures that are required by ISO 9001. The standard requires you to conduct internal audits at defined intervals. The auditors must be trained, and they must not audit their own work. In small organizations it can be a challenge to meet this last requirement, since people often wear more than one hat. One of the easiest ways to accomplish this is to have people who work in the office and generally handle purchasing, customer service, engineering, and accounting functions do the audits of production, receiving, warehousing, and shipping. The individuals who are usually out on the production floor get to audit purchasing, quoting and order processing, management review, and training. Having several people trained as auditors facilitates your ability to get full coverage.

Your audit schedule should reflect the importance of processes and, over time, the results of previous audits. If the workforce is stable and the processes are mature, it may be appropriate to only audit the training processes once a year. However, if you have a lot of turnover or the nature of your product requires constant revisions to processes, then you might want to audit these activities more frequently.

As mentioned in Chapter 6, the output of these audits is one of the inputs into management review. The audit report is the output of this process. It should provide information about:

- Problems that require action

- Risks and potential problems that should be analyzed and addressed

- Opportunities for improvement

- Benchmarks that can be used to improve other processes

The standard requires that action be taken on identified nonconformances through correction or corrective action that addresses the problems and their causes. Records must be maintained of the internal audit reports and resulting actions.

Monitoring and Measurement of Processes

Monitoring of processes does not need to be complicated. And the standard only requires measurement where it is applicable. The monitoring of activities should result in a demonstration that the processes are effective in achieving the required outputs. In some cases there will be overlap between this requirement and the next one, which relates to the monitoring of product. In many instances it's appropriate to infer that if the process is shown to be capable and effective, the resulting product should conform to requirements. So monitoring the process helps to ensure product conformity. Here are some ways of confirming that the output of the process meets requirements:

- Records of first-piece approval show that the job setup process is effective and the rest of the pieces that are produced should be to spec

- Double-checking orders before they're issued to the floor verifies that the information is correct

- A second checkmark on the packing slip shows that the items that were picked are the ones that went into the shipping container

- Gages on equipment show that the required pressure to achieve acceptable product is being maintained

- Signatures on a production traveler indicate that processes were conducted in accordance with specified requirements

- Time studies show that services are being performed within the allocated time

The value of monitoring processes is that you get to catch mistakes and take action before the problem reaches the customer.

This requirement dovetails with the two previous requirements: quality objectives and process performance as an input to management review. The effectiveness of your processes is directly linked to your ability to serve your customers. The degree to which you've been able to achieve objectives related to those processes is a measure of improvement, ROI for resources expended, and, ultimately, how well you're doing overall.

Monitoring and Measurement of Product

It's important to verify that the product conforms to requirements. This is done through inspections, tests, reviews, verifications, and any other methods that allow you to conclude that the product is okay to ship or the service has been provided in accordance with customer requirements.

In a manufacturing environment this is generally done through in-process and/or final inspections and tests. The product is verified using mechanical gages, comparators, test fixtures, and so forth. In some cases the product is a report—for example, the output from a forensic lab, calibration service, or medical lab. In these instances, an authorized signature denoting review signifies acceptance. For software, the product acceptance may be built into the validation process.

In each instance the product is determined to conform to requirements, it is released for delivery by authorized individuals, and evidence of the acceptance is maintained.

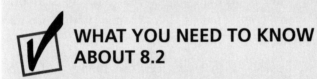

WHAT YOU NEED TO KNOW ABOUT 8.2

You must:

- Assess customer satisfaction

- Conduct internal audits at defined intervals using trained auditors

- Take action on findings from audits

- Monitor processes to make sure things are working in accordance with defined requirements

- Monitor and measure product to ensure it conforms to requirements

- Ensure that product release is done by authorized individuals

- Maintain appropriate records

8.3 CONTROL OF NONCONFORMING PRODUCT

This process is another on the list of ISO 9001 requirements for a documented procedure. The organization is required to identify and control product that does not conform to requirements so it doesn't get shipped to the customer.

Identification can be achieved through colored stickers, tags, or reports affixed to the material. You can control nonconforming product by segregating it from other material or by locating and identifying it so clearly that everyone knows it is not acceptable for use. Materials may also be placed on designated shelves or in specially colored bins to denote their status and to prevent unintended use. The single most important thing to remember is that you must protect against the material being incorporated into a product or the product being delivered to a customer.

The next thing covered in this clause is what to do with the nonconforming material. As appropriate to your industry, these are some of the options:

- Repair or rework the product to bring it into conformity (when material is reworked or repaired, it has to be reinspected or reverified)

- Release the material to the customer, once they have authorized the concession (for example, if the thickness tolerance for material is 8 mil ± 1, the customer would agree to accept any material that is up to 10 mil, but not over 10)

- Prevent its original use (for example, regrading for use, selling to a different market, scrapping or destroying)

The organization also has to address the contingency that a product defect may not be detected until after the product has shipped. This is handled through such activities as repair, retrofit, recall, or replacement. In all instances, actions must clearly be approved by authorized individuals and records maintained.

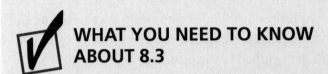

WHAT YOU NEED TO KNOW ABOUT 8.3

You must:

- Identify and control nonconforming material

- Take action to prevent its unintended use

- Rework the material, get a concession from the customer, or take action (such as destruction) to prevent its original use

- Reinspect product that is reworked or repaired

- Ensure that disposition of material is approved by authorized individuals

- Take appropriate action if a defect is discovered after the product is delivered

- Keep records of actions taken

8.4 ANALYSIS OF DATA

This clause is really a reiteration of what's been mentioned in several different areas. You need to analyze the data from the monitoring and measurement activities. This is particularly useful in identifying trends. It helps to ensure that you can make decisions based on good objective data. It enables the actions that are described in the continual improvement clause that follows.

The data to be analyzed come from four general inputs. The first three are mentioned earlier in this chapter. The fourth is discussed in Chapter 8 in the section on purchasing. The four inputs are:

- Customer satisfaction
- Conformity to product requirements
- Characteristics and trends of processes
- Suppliers

Looking at this requirement in terms of others that have already been discussed, the sequence of processes might go like this:

- Monitor and measure processes and products
- Gather data about the results of the monitoring and measuring
- Analyze the information
- Review the information either at the departmental level or at management review
- Review and adjust any objectives relating to the data gathered
- Take action to improve
- Restart the cycle of monitoring

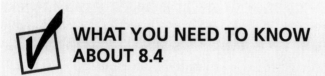

WHAT YOU NEED TO KNOW ABOUT 8.4

You must:

- Gather and analyze data relating to customer satisfaction, process and product conformance, and suppliers
- Use the output of the analysis for continual improvement

8.5 CONTINUAL IMPROVEMENT

Based on all that has come before, it's apparent that the expectation is for the organization to improve its products and processes over time. In addition to any improvement initiatives that ensue from data analysis, establishment of objectives, internal audits, and management review, ISO 9001:2008 specifies two processes that are relevant to an organization's ability to achieve continual improvement. They are corrective action and preventive action. These processes are the last two on the list of required documented procedures.

Corrective Action

This part of the standard requires you to review nonconformities, investigate their cause, decide what action is appropriate, implement that action, record the results, and review the effectiveness of the action taken. The intent of the requirement is that the action taken not only fixes the existing problem but addresses the cause so that the problem or defect does not recur.

The first paragraph contains one of the most ignored "shalls" in the entire standard. It states: "Corrective actions shall be appropriate to the effects of the nonconformities encountered." What that means is that you don't always have to take corrective action. Defects and glitches that have no appreciable effect on processes or the resulting product may not warrant corrective action. In those instances, correction may be a viable option. *Correction* is defined in ISO 9000:2005 as "action to eliminate a detected nonconformity." Sometimes it's just a matter of fixing the defect and moving on.

Understanding the effect of the nonconformity is what helps you decide what to do. So this particular "shall" requires you to do some kind of evaluation so that you can determine whether conducting corrective action is the appropriate thing to do. For example, say there's a mar on the back of a cabinet that will be installed into a piece of equipment. The mar is definitely a nonconformance. However, both you and the customer agree that since the defect is only cosmetic and will not be seen by anyone, it's not worth the time and resources it will take to investigate the root cause and then develop and implement a corrective action plan. Conversely, we can look at an example where the consequences would be significantly different. Let's say a company manufactures small fasteners that go into an implantable medical device. Despite the fact that the company makes tens of thousands of these items, it can't afford to have any defects. It only takes one bad fastener to cause a device to fail, resulting in injury or death. In this case, despite the fact that the small part may only cost about 10 cents, not doing corrective action might cost someone's life.

Conducting a brief or rudimentary evaluation of a situation allows an organization to focus on the nonconformities that are causing the most serious problems, creating the most risk for customers, and ultimately costing the most money.

Once a decision is made to initiate a corrective action, the following steps must be taken:

- Conduct a thorough root cause analysis to discover the real cause—or causes. The cause may relate to a process that is several steps removed from the point of discovery. For instance, a defect may be discovered during field replacement. However, the ultimate root cause is not that the field technician screwed up; it's that the people at headquarters did not update this individual's field manual and work instructions for the latest version of the product. In this case, the root cause lies with the process for distributing documentation.

  There are many tools and techniques you can avail yourself of to conduct root cause analysis. What they all have in common is the essential need to understand the breakdown in the process that ultimately caused the problem.

- Develop and implement an action plan that will address the cause. This may involve several activities such as making changes to a process, revising documents, acquiring tools and equipment, and training key personnel on the changes. Ensure that the plan is clearly defined, that it is assigned to qualified individuals, and that there are adequate resources.

- Once the plan is implemented, it's important to review the action taken and determine its effectiveness. How will you know that the plan worked and that it was successful in preventing recurrence?

   One of the easiest ways of verifying effectiveness is to review records similar to the ones that allowed you to originally detect the problem. For example, if customers returned product due to excessive noise, then it would be appropriate to check (after the corrective action plan has been in place for several months) to see if there has been a recurrence of the same complaint.

You might also consider doing an additional internal audit of the processes that are relevant to that particular customer or product. Finally, it's also beneficial, although not a requirement, to include in the follow-up an assessment of any money that has been saved as a result of the action taken. Going back to the noisy product example, if every return of this nature cost the organization $4000 in rework, scrap, and administrative costs, and if it happened an average of six times per quarter, then implementing a corrective action costing $3,500 (which would prevent recurrence) would net the organization an ROI of $20,500 (see Figure 9.1).

Preventive Action

This last subclause of the standard requires organizations to address potential problems and their causes. Its placement at

Quarterly cost of problem

Incident costs:

Material scrap	$1,200
Labor/machine time	$2,200
Administrative costs	$600
Total cost per incident:	$4,000
Cost of six incidents per quarter:	$24,000

Cost of corrective action

Preventive action costs:

New tooling	$1,600
Time to reengineer process	$900
Time to revise documents	$500
Training on new process	$500
Total cost of corrective action:	$3,500

Return on investment

Incident cost per quarter − corrective action cost = $20,500

Figure 9.1   Example of return on investment for effective corrective action.

the end of ISO 9001 is unfortunate because preventive action is *not* the sequel to corrective action. In fact, the better job you do of preventive action, the fewer corrective actions you will have to do. Whereas corrective action is a reactive process, preventive action is a proactive process.

Ultimately, preventive action is a matter of how we manage change and the consequence of change. We consider what could go wrong, we investigate what would cause that something to go wrong, and then we take appropriate action to prevent its occurrence:

- For a product redesign, we consider whether changing one component will have an adverse effect on how other parts work

- If a storeroom is messy, we rearrange the area to prevent the loss of inventory or time wasted hunting for parts

- If schedules will be affected by the switch to daylight savings time, we set up a system to review all field service that will occur on that day

Some examples of preventive action tools are:

- Failure modes and effects analysis (FMEA)

- Risk management

- Poka-yoke

- Lean initiatives

Preventive actions aren't complicated. Organizations often conduct more of them than they record, which is regrettable because they often contain good ideas that can be transferred to other departments or facilities.

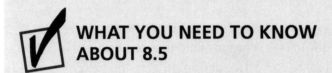

WHAT YOU NEED TO KNOW ABOUT 8.5

You must:

- Improve products and processes

- Conduct corrective actions to address the cause of problems in order to prevent their recurrence

- Conduct preventive actions to address the cause of potential problems in order to prevent their occurrence

- Keep records of actions taken

- Determine the effectiveness of the action taken

Appendix

Related ISO Standards from TC 176

These standards provide guidance and may help you to better understand how to implement certain aspects of your QMS and how to get additional benefit from implementing and maintaining it.

ISO 9000:2005	*Quality management systems— Fundamentals and vocabulary*
ISO 9004:2009	*Managing for the sustained success of an organization—A quality management approach*
ISO 10001:2007	*Quality management—Customer satisfaction—Guidelines for codes of conduct for organizations*
ISO 10002:2004	*Quality management—Customer satisfaction—Guidelines for complaints handling in organizations*
ISO 10003:2007	*Quality management—Customer satisfaction—Guidelines for dispute resolution external to organizations*
ISO/TS 10004:2010	*Quality management—Customer satisfaction—Guidelines for monitoring and measuring*

ISO 10005:2005	*Quality management systems—Guidelines for quality plans*
ISO 10006:2003	*Quality management systems—Guidelines for quality management in projects*
ISO 10007:2003	*Quality management systems—Guidelines for configuration management*
ISO 10012:2003	*Measurement management systems—Requirements for measurement processes and measuring equipment*
ISO/TR 10013:2001	*Guidelines for quality management system documentation*
ISO 10014:2006	*Quality management—Guidelines for realizing financial and economic benefits*
ISO 10015:1999	*Quality management—Guidelines for training*
ISO/TR 10017:2003	*Guidance on statistical techniques for ISO 9001:2000*
ISO 10019:2005	*Guidelines for the selection of quality management system consultants and use of their services*
ISO/TS 16949:2009	*Quality management systems—Particular requirements for the application of ISO 9001:2008 for automotive production and relevant service part organizations*
ISO 19011:2002	*Guidelines for quality and/or environmental management systems auditing*

Index

Belong to the Quality Community!

Established in 1946, ASQ is a global community of quality experts in all fields and industries. ASQ is dedicated to the promotion and advancement of quality tools, principles, and practices in the workplace and in the community.

The Society also serves as an advocate for quality. Its members have informed and advised the U.S. Congress, government agencies, state legislatures, and other groups and individuals worldwide on quality-related topics.

Vision

By making quality a global priority, an organizational imperative, and a personal ethic, ASQ becomes the community of choice for everyone who seeks quality technology, concepts, or tools to improve themselves and their world.

ASQ is...

- More than 90,000 individuals and 700 companies in more than 100 countries
- The world's largest organization dedicated to promoting quality
- A community of professionals striving to bring quality to their work and their lives
- The administrator of the Malcolm Baldrige National Quality Award
- A supporter of quality in all sectors including manufacturing, service, healthcare, government, and education
- YOU

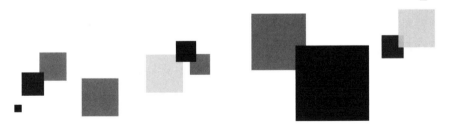

Visit www.asq.org for more information.

ASQ Membership

Research shows that people who join associations experience increased job satisfaction, earn more, and are generally happier*. ASQ membership can help you achieve this while providing the tools you need to be successful in your industry and to distinguish yourself from your competition. So why wouldn't you want to be a part of ASQ?

Networking

Have the opportunity to meet, communicate, and collaborate with your peers within the quality community through conferences and local ASQ section meetings, ASQ forums or divisions, ASQ Communities of Quality discussion boards, and more.

Professional Development

Access a wide variety of professional development tools such as books, training, and certifications at a discounted price. Also, ASQ certifications and the ASQ Career Center help enhance your quality knowledge and take your career to the next level.

Solutions

Find answers to all your quality problems, big and small, with ASQ's Knowledge Center, mentoring program, various e-newsletters, *Quality Progress* magazine, and industry-specific products.

Access to Information

Learn classic and current quality principles and theories in ASQ's Quality Information Center (QIC), *ASQ Weekly* e-newsletter, and product offerings.

Advocacy Programs

ASQ helps create a better community, government, and world through initiatives that include social responsibility, Washington advocacy, and Community Good Works.

Visit www.asq.org/membership for more information on ASQ membership.

*2008, The William E. Smith Institute for Association Research

ASQ Certification

ASQ certification is formal recognition by ASQ that an individual has demonstrated a proficiency within, and comprehension of, a specified body of knowledge at a point in time. Nearly 150,000 certifications have been issued. ASQ has members in more than 100 countries, in all industries, and in all cultures. ASQ certification is internationally accepted and recognized.

Benefits to the Individual

- New skills gained and proficiency upgraded
- Investment in your career
- Mark of technical excellence
- Assurance that you are current with emerging technologies
- Discriminator in the marketplace
- Certified professionals earn more than their uncertified counterparts
- Certification is endorsed by more than 125 companies

Benefits to the Organization

- Investment in the company's future
- Certified individuals can perfect and share new techniques in the workplace
- Certified staff are knowledgeable and able to assure product and service quality

Quality is a global concept. It spans borders, cultures, and languages. No matter what country your customers live in or what language they speak, they demand quality products and services. You and your organization also benefit from quality tools and practices. Acquire the knowledge to position yourself and your organization ahead of your competition.

CERTIFICATIONS INCLUDE

- Biomedical Auditor – CBA
- Calibration Technician – CCT
- HACCP Auditor – CHA
- Pharmaceutical GMP Professional – CPGP
- Quality Inspector – CQI
- Quality Auditor – CQA
- Quality Engineer – CQE
- Quality Improvement Associate – CQIA
- Quality Technician – CQT
- Quality Process Analyst – CQPA
- Reliability Engineer – CRE
- Six Sigma Black Belt – CSSBB
- Six Sigma Green Belt – CSSGB
- Software Quality Engineer – CSQE
- Manager of Quality/Organizational Excellence – CMQ/OE

ASQ Training

Classroom-based Training

ASQ offers training in a traditional classroom setting on a variety of topics. Our instructors are quality experts and lead courses that range from one day to four weeks, in several different cities. Classroom-based training is designed to improve quality and your organization's bottom line. Benefit from quality experts; from comprehensive, cutting-edge information; and from peers eager to share their experiences.

Web-based Training

VIRTUAL COURSES

ASQ's virtual courses provide the same expert instructors, course materials, interaction with other students, and ability to earn CEUs and RUs as our classroom-based training, without the hassle and expenses of travel. Learn in the comfort of your own home or workplace. All you need is a computer with Internet access and a telephone.

Self-paced Online Programs

These online programs allow you to work at your own pace while obtaining the quality knowledge you need. Access them whenever it is convenient for you, accommodating your schedule.

SOME TRAINING TOPICS INCLUDE

- Auditing
- Basic Quality
- Engineering
- Education
- Healthcare
- Government
- Food Safety
- ISO
- Leadership
- Lean
- Quality Management
- Reliability
- Six Sigma
- Social Responsibility

Visit www.asq.org/training for more information.